Creating Excellence in Our Schools

. . .by Taking *More* Lessons from America's Best-Run Companies

Creating Excellence in Our Schools

...by Taking *More* Lessons from America's Best-Run Companies

James Lewis, Jr.

J. L. Wilkerson Publishing Company
P.O. Box 948
Westbury, New York

Library of Congress Cataloging in Publishing Data

Lewis, James, Jr., 1930-
Creating excellence in our schools by taking more lessons
    from America's best-run companies

    Bibliography: p.
    Includes Index.
    1. School management and organization—United States
2. School superintendents and principals—United States.
3. Industrial management—United States. 4. Educational
surveys—United States. I. Title.
LB2805.L414   1986   371.2'00973   85-51533
ISBN 0-915253-04-6

To my son
Terence James Lewis
who is finding himself

• Acknowledgements •

I am indebted to a large number of people who helped make this book a reality. I owe a great deal of gratitude to the corporate, school, and community people who shared information and materials with me. These people, many of who must remain anonymous, gave generously of their time and insights.

I would like to thank Thomas and Daisy Eddy for their patience and fortitude in word processing this manuscript. I am deeply indebted to my editor, Quica Ostrander, for her curative insights and superior skills. I am also grateful to Annette Williams, who creatively produced the book jacket.

Finally, I am very appreciative of my family and friends, who understand my champion-like behavior and allow me to exist as I truly am.

James Lewis, Jr.
New York

• Contents •

• Hallmarks of Excellence

The following list of characteristics that distinguish an excellent school district is provided to give you food for thought and action so that you can forge your own path to excellence.

Excellence is:

- A school district in which school administrators have the courage to refrain from rigidly defining jobs and to seek opportunities to share information and exchange ideas with their school people.

- A school district in which each new school person is presented with long-term career-path plan so that he or she is continually challenged to learn to perform multiple jobs.

- A school district in which school administrators are skilled in strategic management and, as a result, strive to get the entire school district to discover and define those values that are shared by all school people, establish a common purpose, and determine specific activities necessary to reach that purpose.

- A school district in which school administrators are taking appropriate actions to inculcate a school culture that capitalizes on school people's quest for self-development.

- A school district in which school administrators are moving from seeking or keeping power to empowering others (that is, from controlling school people to enabling them to be innovative and creative).

- A school district in which school administrators are dedicated to keeping the overall vision of the school organization alive by synthesizing activities and finding order in difficult and complex situations.

- A school district in which school administrators search for harmony, wholeness, consistency, quality, truth, and excellence.

- A school district that recognizes school administrators' achievements in the area of human resources—reducing absenteeism, developing performance skills, resolving school people's grievances, improving the quality of services to kids, etc.

- A school district in which the mission is to provide kids with the finest possible education by developing the potential of school people to fulfill the school district's purposes and mission.

- A school district in which the superintendent believes in the idea of harmony over opposition and strives to foster good union/management relations by sincerely educating the union and school people as to the importance of cooperation.

- A school district in which school administrators feel personally responsible for the welfare of their school people.

It Takes Visionary People to Achieve Excellence

My hobby is sculpture and the process of building a
new car is very much like carving a sculpture. First
you make a total picture in your mind of what it will
be, then you build it.

—Hulki Aldikacti

Almost immediately after the publication of my book
Achieving Excellence in Our Schools, I received letters
and comments from a number of my readers declaring
that the book did not go far enough. They felt that there
were other lessons at least as important as some of those
I had presented for achieving excellence. Therefore, I
prepared a one-page survey and mailed it to over 3500
educators, including superintendents, central administrators, principals, and teachers. The response was
great: 1876 respondents sent back the survey. The results of the survey were the basis for most of the lessons
in *Creating Excellence in Our Schools*.

If you are among the thousands who have picked up
Achieving Excellence in Our Schools, you probably took
one of four courses: you opened the book and read some
pages; you read several chapters and underlined certain

statements; you read the book from cover to cover and made notes on those principles and practices that your school district could implement; or you thoroughly digested the book, began to think about what new ideas you could combine with your own, and took some immediate steps to begin pursuing your path to excellence. Unfortunately, only a small percentage of school people have taken the fourth course. I believe that is because a large majority of the people who have read *Achieving Excellence in Our Schools* have failed to create a vision, a vital prerequisite for achieving excellence. Tom Peters emphasizes the importance of a vision in both of his books, *In Search of Excellence* and *A Passion for Excellence*.

What Is a Vision?

What do I mean by a vision? Basically, a vision is a person's mental image of the future, based on a collection of information, knowledge, ideas, aspirations, dreams, dangers and opportunities.

Creating a vision is a two-stage operation. The first part is the intuitive imagining of a possible desired achievement. The second part is the most difficult yet crucial aspect of planning—converting the intuitive vision into an action plan. These two aspects of creating a vision must be carried out alternately, with the right or creative side of the brain thinking of an ideal to help realize the desired achievement and the left or analytical side of the brain determining the concrete implications of the intuitive vision.

The vision of a superintendent is not simply a vague idea of a desired end, nor is it just a clear picture of a single aspect of a school district. It is an operating model of all aspects of the organization being created and the actual steps necessary to make that model a reality. To pursue excellence, you will need to spend a lot of time building and testing your mental model of excellence. You will need to see kids, curriculum and instructions, finance, administration, research and development, and human resources as an integrated system. The ability to visualize the steps from an idea to realization is one of the most important jobs of a superintendent. *Creating Excellence in Our Schools* will enable you to see the many aspects of the school district as a totality and will provide you with insights so that you can perform with courage and decisiveness the tasks necessary to give life to your vision.

Excellence Cannot Be Narrowly Defined

Far too many school and community people believe that achieving excellence in education merely means making such changes as increasing graduation requirements, beginning certain lessons earlier, abolishing social promotion, upgrading texts, increasing teacher salaries, and increasing scores in reading. I would be the first to say that all of these efforts are important, but excellence must begin with good school management. If we manage our schools by implementing the principles, practices, and programs cited in my two books on excellence, I believe that we are likely to achieve excellence; if, on the other hand, we increase here, abolish there, and upgrade over there, as recommended by various commissions on excellence in education, we have no guarantee that excellence will be achieved or sustained for any length of time. What is needed is for a revolution to take place in education, similar to the one that, according Tom Peters, is taking place in business and industry. He said, "In the private or public sector, big business or small, we observe that there are only two ways to create and sustain superior performance over the long haul. First, take exceptional care of the customers [kids] via superior service and superior quality. Second, certainly innovate. That's it." I have taken the substance of Tom's books and related them to education in an effort to facilitate your pursuit of excellence; the rest is up to you.

The Power of Vision

Even after Beethoven had lost his hearing, he could still test different ideas in his mind. He had a powerful imagination that allowed him to "hear" an entire symphony. What enabled him to be a great musician was in part this extraordinary ability to visualize—or in his case, to "hear" —his symphonies before they were actually performed.

Nikola Tesla, the inventor of three-phase electric current, new turbines, and a number of other inventions, explained how he put his vision to work to make his inventions a reality. He would construct a mental model of the invention. He would "operate" the model mentally and then forget about it for a while. Weeks later he would let the model surface again in his mind and mentally check for wear. If the model wasn't performing properly, he would redesign it mentally, then submerge it in his mind for more mental testing until it operated perfectly. Most engineers would tell you that the testing of an invention is impossible unless one has a general blueprint to see how parts fit together—impossible unless one has the incredibly precise, concrete, and visionary acuity of a Tesla.

In the world of business, when a powerful vision meets its demise because of changing times and conditions, so does the company. For example, VisiCalc's software was at one time the predominant business software—that is, until Lotus Development Corporation successfully implemented founder Mitchell Lapur's vision of user-friendly, "all-in-one" software with Lotus 1-2-3. As a result, Lotus is outselling VisiCalc two to one. Sony Corporation introduced a line of cameras with electronic imaging, which exemplified Sony's vision. Kodak, long the frontrunning company in the photographic field, is now trying to catch up to Sony, all because of one vision that was realized.

Some of the best-known companies faltered because their competitors were more visionary. For example, National Cash Register lacked the vision to move from electro-mechanical cash registers to electronic ones. As a result, in 1970 NCR's competitors came out with new technology that rendered NCR's products obsolete, making it necessary for NCR to write off $140 million in outdated equipment. In 1976, B. F. Goodrich became the principal maker of bias-ply tires in the United States by requiring that its suppliers come up with improved raw materials and its engineers with better designs. However, by 1979 bias-ply tires had become obsolete; Michelin's radial tires had consumed the market. Busy perpetuating the past, Goodrich failed to envision the future, and the company has yet to recuperate from this lack of vision.

Visionary and Nonvisionary Leaders

John Kotter, Harvard Business School professor and author of the *General Manager*, has reported some interesting findings about visionary and nonvisionary managers. He maintains that:

- Visionary managers usually have only a few crucial appointments scheduled on their calendars. On the other hand, nonvisionary managers overload their calendars and are unable to squeeze in any last-minute appointments.

- Visionary managers spend a great deal of time walking around the organization, greeting and talking to people. Nonvisionary managers spend most of their time in large, formal meetings, during which they direct the actions of the staff.

- Visionary managers frequently talk about the philosophy, the directions, and the values they think will help to maintain excellence. Nonvisionary managers seldom talk about a philosophy, and in fact appear not to have one.

- Visionary managers are generally cheerful and optimistic; they encourage their employees to apply both heart and mind to their jobs, because in the critical path of life the two should not be separated. Nonvisionary managers tend to be sulky and rarely smile; they usually will take staff members aside between meetings to criticize their performance.

- During a day on the job, visionary managers spend a lot of time in the plant discussing new products and services. They conduct spontaneous and informal meetings with key people, after which they often will deliver an inspirational speech to small groups of company people. Nonvisionary managers waste much of their time in formal meetings and devote a lot of time to unproductive undertakings, such as reviewing a sales training film strip and reading it aloud to district managers.

Traits of Visionary School Administrators

In their book *Creating Excellence*, Craig R. Hickman and Michael A. Silva use the work of Abraham Zalenik of the Harvard Business School as a basis for formulating some traits of a visionary manager. I have related these traits to educational administrators. Those administrators who rightfully deserve the description of "visionary leaders" are

- Able to search for knowledge, ideas, concepts and ways of thinking until a clear vision crystallizes.

- Keen at articulating the vision into an easy-to-grasp philosophy that integrates strategic direction with the values of the school organization.

- Adept at motivating people to embrace the vision by providing consistent encouragement and by performing as a role model.

- Able to relate to people in a warm, supportive, and expressive way, always communicating to others that "we are a family; what affects one affects all of us."

- Adroit at keeping in contact with all people at every level in the school district in an attempt to understand their concerns and the impact of the vision on them.

- Able to translate the vision so that everyone is able to relate it to his or her own individual interest, concerns, and job.

- Astute at remaining at the core of the action so as to be the primary source for shaping the vision.

- Able to evaluate the progress of the school organization in terms of the degree to which the vision has been actualized.

- Adept at focusing on the major strengths of the school organization in an effort to centralize the vision.

- Cunning in seeking ways to improve, augment, or further develop the vision of the school district by carefully monitoring changes within and outside of the school organization.

All School People Play a Part in Actualizing the Vision

It takes visionary people to achieve excellence in education. The superintendent must conceive of the vision, the board of education must act on the vision, and the school people must perform harmoniously to actualize the vision. If any one of these stages is poorly executed, the goal of excellence in education is lost. Therefore, the superintendent is the key; he or she must have the knowledge and skills necessary to create a vision that when actualized will produce excellence. However, if the board of education is bent on mediocrity and does not have the guts to do what is necessary to help navigate the school district in the direction of excellence, the superintendent's vision will not be actualized. Finally, if the superintendent has created a sound vision for the school district and the board of education has acted in a meaningful manner on the recommendations of the superintendent but school people are not managed and organized in an appropriate manner, the vision will not be actualized and the school district will continue to perpetuate the status quo. *Achieving Excellence in Our Schools* and *Creating Excellence in Our Schools* provide the kind of information and knowledge necessary for the superintendent to arrive at a vision that has a high probability of becoming a reality. These two books offer board members the most current knowledge available about how to manage a school district, knowledge that will enable them to make sound decisions. And these two books are invaluable guides to school administrators and other school people in that they provide practical guidelines so that everyone can work cooperatively in an effort to achieve all goals, objectives, and activities designed to actualize the vision.

The board of education and superintendent must have as their common quest the pursuit of educational excellence. The superintendent must dramatize the vision to school people. In essence, the superintendent must be what Tom Peters and Nancy Austin call the "chief salesperson." It is the superintendent's role to teach school administrators what the school district is going to do to work toward excellence, and to get the school administrators to teach that vision to their people.

The best way to teach the vision is simply and directly. Tell everybody in and out of the school district about the district's quest for excellence. What steps are presently being taken? How long will the quest take? What evidence will indicate that the vision is becoming a reality? The superintendent must embody the dreams, values, and aspirations of the school district. He or she must be a true believer and must characterize that vision through his or her words, actions, deeds, and thoughts.

During my tenure as superintendent of schools, there were several occasions in which the fuel that propelled me to actualize my achievements was a vision. I shall describe two instances.

The first occurred almost immediately after I took my first job as superintendent of schools, in a poor community. My vision was to find a way for any graduating students or adults in the community who wished to pursue higher education to do so without paying for it. I discussed my vision with the school board prior to and after assuming my new role, and the board agreed to let me try. I contacted Harry Wofford, who was president of the Old Westbury College of the State University of New York. He and his staff established a cordial relationship with my administrative team. He and his top-level administrators would visit my school district, and my team and I would visit the college. When, I mentioned my vision to Harry, he and his staff became enthusiastic about it. He set the forces into motion to enable some of his staff to work with mine to put substance on the bones of my vision. He made contact with people he knew at the state level and got them interested. My vision was beginning to blossom, and I ventured to discuss with Harry and my board of education the need to find someone to pursue it fulltime—someone who was an excellent humanist as well as an excellent manager, someone who could run with an idea and fully actualize the vision. We had the good fortune to find such a person, and we hired him. The fine job he did in actualizing this vision far exceeded my expectations. He made arrangements so that both graduating seniors and adults could attend the Wyandanch College Center for a period of two years without paying for books and could be admitted to Old Westbury College to complete their junior and senior years in order to attain their undergraduate degree. Two significant things occurred as a result of this vision: First, graduating seniors and hundreds of community people received a college education, which in all likelihood they would not have done if it had not been convenient for them; and second, the success of the program led to its being spread throughout the state.

My second vision took hold when I realized how poorly my students were reading. On the state-wide reading test they scored at the seventeenth percentile in reading. At first I attempted to deal with our reading problem by trying out other reading programs to determine which one would give us maximum results. I soon realized that this plan was not working. One day I happened to be in Newark, New Jersey, and decided to visit the Morton Street School to see one of my childhood friends, George Cureton. When I visited George's first-grade class, I noticed that an extremely large number of his students were reading at second- and third-grade level. I was amazed. I knew then that I had found the way to actualize my vision. Coincidentally, George was going on sabbatical leave for a period of one year. I persuaded him to serve as a consultant and trainer in my school district while on sabbatical, and to teach and supervise four kindergarten and first-grade classes in order to determine the effects of using his reading program in my district. The board approved my plan, and the experiment was set in motion for one year. The results were outstanding. No other reading program in the school district had nearly the success of George's reading program. In fact, as a result of the pilot program, all kindergarten students were reading at a first-grade level or above, and some were reading at a third-grade level. Members of the school board were elated. I persuaded George to take a leave of absence after his sabbatical and work in the school district as a full-time trainer and consultant. At this point I had completed the first two important steps in actualizing my vision: I conceptualized the vision, and I had aligned myself with people who could help me actualize my vision.

The next step was full-scale implementation. By closely monitoring the pilot program, I found one flaw in the manner in which the program was being implemented. It needed to be structured. So I assigned my director of curriculum and instructions the task of working with our reading supervisor to prepare a reading program curriculum which would also be used as a training guide.

After structure had been given to the reading program, I met with all elementary teachers and principals. I informed them that we had a serious problem in reading and described the unsuccessful attempts that had been made to improve our reading scores. Then I indicated that since this problem had existed in our school district for countless years, I was declaring on this day a state of emergency. I asked the school board to approve the implementation of the Cureton reading program and the elimination of all other reading programs. I then announced that all elementary teachers and teacher aides, all elementary principals, and I would be required to undergo one month of training in the Cureton reading program. During the month we all would receive training in the morning and would work on the practical application of that training in the afternoon session with the kids. I explained that teachers had a choice of taking the training during either July or August, and that everyone would be adequately compensated for the training. I believe that what gave impetus to my vision was the fact that I attended the training sessions with the teachers and taught the program along with them. We all worked together to materialize my vision. The program was implemented not only on the elementary level but also on the intermediate level. The results were outstanding. On the state-wide reading test, the district's primary scores jumped from the seventeenth percentile to the eighty-third percentile. When the success of the new reading program made the services of the thirteen remedial reading teachers unnecessary, I simply did not renew their contracts. My vision had been actualized. Looking back on my plans to actualize my vision, I have one regret—I wish I had been more sensitive to the needs of my remedial reading teachers. I should have located positions for them in the school district.

After relating the success of the reading program to a group of superintendents, Marcus Foster, the late superintendent of the Oakland, California, School District, said, "With your kind of enthusiasm, Jim, any program can work." I believe he was saying, in essence, that when you create a vision and have a strong desire to actualize it, almost any program can be successful. This is what excellence is about.

Strategies for Achieving Excellence

- Use the characteristics of a visionary school administrator described in this book to develop an instrument for assessing educational leaders. Use a rating system from 1 to 50, with 50 being the highest rating. A perfect rating of 50 will identify fully visionary educational leaders. A score below 30 will indicate that improvement is needed.

- Convene a three- to five-day conference with your key school and community people, and together consider the following questions:

— What are the principles and practices of the revolution in U.S. management? Are they applicable to education? Which ones are feasible for us to adopt?

— What do our kids want? Do they value what we do for them? Can we enhance our value? How should we change our curriculum to fortify them for the future?

— What do we do well? What do we do poorly? How can we improve? What constrictions keep us from improving?

— What is our potential? Where could we be in five or ten years?

— Why have we succeeded or failed in the past? Do we really understand the reasons for our success or failure? Are we being honest with ourselves?

— If we could rewrite our school district's history, what would we change?

These are only a few of the vital questions that should
be posed for the group to ponder in developing the vision.
Others should be explored. Each question should be
explored in depth, and a final consensus should be
reached and written down. It may be wise to hire a
professional facilitator to spend a few days in the school
district prior to facilitating the group.

- Involve all school people in helping you to arrive at
  your vision. Circulate a memo to call schools requesting that they identify something within the
  school district that they would improve if it were
  left up to them. When all the responses have been
  received, rank the items, preferably through use of
  a computer. Critically review all of the responses,
  regardless of rank. Arrive at a shared vision by
  involving others, such as the administrative team,
  in formulating the final vision. Prepare a written
  statement of the vision, and thank the respondents
  for their participation in arriving at the shared
  vision statement.

- Regardless of the manner in which you develop
  your vision, do the following to give life to your
  vision:

— Concentrate on the key elements of the vision.

— Stay deeply involved at the core of things so that
  you can initiate appropriate actions to actualize
  the vision.

— Induce all people to embrace the vision.

— Always look for opportunities to articulate the

vision so that it is inculcated throughout the school and community.

- Using the following guidelines, develop an action plan for actualizing your vision:

— Write a scenario to describe your vision for the school district. Make certain it contains the definition of the vision; identification of opportunities, problems and dangers; a description of key success factors; and the sequence of major events. Distribute this scenario to all administrators and use the document to "poeticize" your vision for the school district.

— Identify people who will help you to actualize your vision. Meet with them frequently to discuss progress toward the vision and additional steps to be taken.

— Describe programs, practices, and principles that will give school people "ownership" in, or a feeling of responsibility for, the vision, and take appropriate action.

— Establish an organizational structure that will help you to actualize your vision. Review your communication approaches and identify ways of improving them to help actualize the vision.

• Lesson 1 •

Attain Excellence Through Ownership.

The power that can be unleashed by a request of "mere" ownership, or even the perception of it, is awesome.
—Tom Peters and Nancy Austin

A teacher who feels that he or she is alive and growing on the job in school will feel that he or she has some ownership in the school. I don't mean ownership in terms of possessing the school, but rather in terms of being responsible for the job he or she holds. A teacher needs to know that on any given day he or she might become a winner by successfully teaching a concept or helping a student with a problem. Teachers want feed back when a job is well done or not well done. Too often teachers feel that they have been deserted, and all they have to do is show up for school. School administrators can no longer expect teachers merely to perform the act of teaching; administrators must solicit teachers' creative input into decision making and their commitment to plans. School administrators therefore need to refrain from rigidly defining teachers' jobs; instead, they must give them access to information, provide them with greater opportunities for exchanging ideas, and enable them to make decisions and execute plans and activities

1

that will help them achieve excellence. The most effective and powerful way to do this is by giving teachers a sense of ownership in the performance of their jobs.

Understanding Why People Reject Imposed Change

To understand what ownership is, you must understand the phenomenon of personal goal fulfillment and the three human addictions. Every human being is endowed from birth with the propensity to fulfill his or her personal goals. In fact, an individual's personal goals take precedence over other important things in life, including spouse, children, and parents. Whenever a person is asked to perform a specific act, the conscious mind quickly determines whether the act is compatible with the person's own goals. If not, the act may not be performed. I say "may not" because the person requesting the act has two alternatives: to abandon the request or to influence the person to modify his or her personal goal in order to make them consonant with the act. The second alternative is called inducing motivation; the aim is to see that one person's personal goals are integrated with the goals of the other person.

Often school administrators influence people to perform an act without taking the time to get the goals integrated. This can have harmful effects on the school administrator and the school district because if a person's personal goals are ignored, they may come to include "getting back at" the school administrator. The process of goal integration seems to be misunderstood by countless numbers of school administrators throughout the country. When I give a seminar or workshop, I usually give the participants a 15-item true-and-false quiz to test their awareness of the latest concepts and theories about school administration. For more than ten years I have given this quiz, and no one has received a satisfactory rating, which is a minimum of 11 correct answers not even professors of education, assistant commissioners of education, superintendents, and other school administrators. There are two statements that most of the respondents mark incorrectly: (1) "The personal goals of teachers take precedence over the goals of school administrators;" and (2) "I don't work for the school district, I work in the school district to fulfill my personal goals. As long as I support the school district, I will be given the opportunity to remain in the school district to fulfill my personal goals." Both of these statements are true. What is interesting is that a large number of teachers tend to get both of them right. A school administrator who does not understand or believe that people's personal goals take precedence over all other goals does not understand his or her real role as an integrator of personal and school organizational goals.

All human beings are afflicted with three addictions: sensation, security, and power. The most influential addiction is security. Any person or any thing that threatens a person's security is met with suspicion, resistance, and at times even force. Whenever people become acclimated to a certain environment or condition, they tend to be satisfied, because when they know what to expect from the environment or condition, their security is not threatened. However, if anyone of the variables that produced the environment is changed, people become dissatisfied and may precipitate some sort of action against the change by directing their personal goals toward sabotaging the change, subverting authority, etc. Therefore, to get people to accept change, we must do two things. First, we must integrate their personal goals with whatever goals we desire to attain. Second, as we do so, we must consider people's security addiction. The best way to facilitate change is by enabling people to effect the change themselves, through the psychology-of-ownership principle.

The Psychology-of-Ownership Principle

The psychology-of-ownership is based on a sense of possession that a person feels as a result of his or her meaningful participation in deciding on and executing an act—a sense of "ownership" of the act. The act must be planned, controlled, and performed in order to be considered meaningful. The act could be the production of a product, the development of a program, the institution of a method, the establishment of a practice, or the solution to a problem. In planning, controlling, and carrying out an act, the person will usually experience a sense of accomplishment and elevated self-esteem. The key to implementing the psychology-of-ownership principle is getting school administrators out of the way of teachers and other school people and giving them leeway to perform in ways that are meaningful to them.

The Meaning of Ownership

When the psychology of ownership is a well-established principle in a school district, the following assumptions will be accepted implicitly.

- Every employee is a manager and will be permitted to plan, control, and perform his or her job.

4

- School people are to be trusted to do what ever is necessary to perform their jobs properly.

- School administrators are to be trusted, too.

- The way a job is performed will be left up to the discretion of the person performing the job, with constraints brought to his or her attention prior to the performance of the job.

- School administrators will make certain that information flows up, down, and sideways throughout the organization, and will convey information to school people so that they can make informed decisions about and on aspects of the school that are directly vital to them.

- School administrators will refrain from rigidly defining school people's jobs.

- School administrators must convey more information to school people so that they are smarter decision makers about aspects of the school directly vital to them.

- School people will be trained to perform in different capacities and positions.

- All performance will be recognized.

- School people will be endowed with autonomy and encouraged to engage in intrapreneurship from their first day in school.

Benefits Associated with Ownership

There are some enormous benefits associated with the psychology-of-ownership principle when it is imple-

5

mented correctly. In fact, I don't know of a single principle or practice that is more effective in enabling a school district to achieve excellence. Following are some of the benefits.

- School people are more inclined to plan and control change; therefore, there is a greater commitment to plans.
- School people are inclined to go beyond the call of duty to perform an act.
- Schools are able to run themselves more efficiently and effectively.
- Enhanced teamwork is exhibited whereby everybody works together to achieve goals.
- Employee problems are solved with less difficulty because peers are involved in the decision making-process.
- Quality and productivity are improved.
- School people experience elevated self-esteem.
- School administrators' jobs are made easier.
- More problems are solved.
- There is a greater satisfaction and improved morale throughout the school organization.

The Power of Ownership in Business

In order to demonstrate the power of the psychology of ownership, I will describe how some companies have been using this principle. Monarch Marking is the maker of labels for retailers. Prior to 1983, one of its divisions was in a state of rapid decline, its sales having fallen from $9 million to $4 million over a three-year period. In 1983, a new manager took over the division and instituted a number of changes. Each week partnership meetings were held, which everyone was required to attend and participate in. Everyone—regardless of his or her position—was treated as a full-scale business partner. Everyone was requested to visit customers regularly. As a result of the new manager's introduction of management through ownership, people began to feel that Monarch was their company and their business. They began to feel better about themselves and more responsible for serving their customers better. The manager made a habit of giving out tokens of excellence, in the form of silver dollars, to declare his gratitude and appreciation.

Tupperware's several hundred distributors have a weekly program called "Rally." At Rally all sales persons participate in a ceremony known as "Count Up," in which they march up front to applause when the account of their personal sales for the week is announced. For example, when $300,000 to $500,000 is read out, those salespersons who have sales falling within that range get up out of their seats and march up front. "Count Up" continues until only the top five salespersons remain seated. These high performers individually march up to the front of the room and sign their names on a high blackboard where their sales figures are listed. Tom Peters and Nancy Austin maintain that for these top five salespersons to sign their names to their sales figures represents the essence of ownership.

At People Express everybody is a manager. In June 1982, this airline company divided its employees into the following categories.

Custom Service Managers
Flight Managers
Maintenance Managers
General Managers
Managing Officers
Team Managers

In this company, there are no sections and no supervisors. Employees function as teams, and every team is expected to manage itself. At People Express the ownership principle is practiced by requiring no rigid job slots; the company encourages its people to look for work and to do their best. The pilot who flew from Washington to New York may be at work the following day in headquarters or marketing. The flight manager who collects fares on board the plane may be working in scheduling the following week. The belief at People Express is that every person working in the airline should be familiar with all jobs in the company. With only a few exceptions, you will not find employees at People Express, but owners.

When Trust House Forte acquired three grand hotels in Paris, the union fought viciously to avoid a foreign takeover. Upon assuming control of one of the hotels, Forte learned that management had effectively left day-to-day operation of the hotel to the union. Forte offered the management post to the shop steward, who happened to be the chief concierge. This new manager introduced an employee participation-ownership program. One feature of the program was that an employee-consultant committee took over the problems of lateness, absenteeism, and other disciplinary matters. In addition, an incentive program was worked out to allow the employees to share with the company all profits above 5 percent of turnover. As a result of these moves, there was a 20 percent decline in staff problems, and profit increased dramatically to to three-and-a-half times what it had been when the hotels were acquired. Employees saw their income quadruple over a five-year period.

H. H. Robertson is a highly profitable British specialty steel producer. The company's managing director felt that the company was missing orders that it should have acquired, so in 1982 he took a radical step to change things. He established a "ginger group" program, whereby *ad hoc* groups were organized to complete a specific project or to accommodate a possible order. Each group consisted of the key people concerned with a given project, regardless of their jobs. For example, a team might consist of people in design, sales, production, cost accounting, and purchasing. Everybody needed to own a piece of the project and was assigned to an ad hoc group. This program has been extremely effective because it has broken down the traditional organizational barriers that usually stifle freedom and creativity. Some companies go to extremes to ensure not only a feeling of ownership in the work environment but stock ownership as well. Companies such as W. C. Gore & Associates, Operations Research Incorporated, Atari, Lowe's Companies, and Denver Yellow Cabs have had remarkable success when they offered stock to their employees to make them owners. Consider the following:

- W. L. Gore & Associates, developers of Gor-Tek and other high-technology products, is run substantially by its people. Its employees have no specific job titles and no conventional hierarchy. Since 1977, this company has been growing at a compound rate of 40 percent yearly.

- Operational Research Incorporated, a 650-employee consulting firm, has seen sales quadruple since 1976, when it became employee-owned.

- Norman Bushwell, the founder of Atari, was able to reduce theft considerably when employees became owners.

- Lowe's Companies, a 7000-employee chain of home improvement stores, found that when the percentage of employee ownership declined significantly, so did production. And when employee ownership increased, so did performance.

- Denver Yellow Cabs, a 1000 employee company, has compiled the nation's best safety record for cab companies since it became employee-owned in 1980.

Ownership Works in Education, Too

Twice during my tenure as a school administrator the psychology-of-ownership not only made my job easier but also produced better results than I could have by myself.

When I became the principal of a brand new middle school, one of my first jobs was to prepare a duty schedule for my teachers. I did what most principals do: I identified all of the times in which teachers have to assume lunch, yard, and hall duties, and assigned teachers to these tasks. When I presented my "duty schedule" to the teachers, they did not voice any disapproval in my presence. However, once I left the scene, I was told, "all hell broke out." I immediately sat down and wrote a list of constraints regarding the duty schedule and gave this list to the brave soul who dared to approach me with the teachers grievances. I told him to take the list of con-

10

straints, and ask the teachers to comply with these constraints in preparing their own duty schedule. Within a few hours I received a teacher-made duty schedule that met all of the constraints, and I was assured that all teachers were satisfied with the new schedule. The result of this approach was that all of the teachers were happy, I was elated because I had thought of the idea, and a duty schedule was produced which all teachers were committed to uphold. When I became superintendent of a small school district, I wanted to establish a model school, one that would feature differentiated staffing, and modular scheduling and be infused with a nongraded and humanistic approach to education. I went to one of the elementary principals and told him what I wanted and how I would like to go about doing it, but only if he was totally committed to my idea. He said he liked the idea and was willing to give it a try. A meeting was scheduled with the teachers. This is what I told them: "I am interested in establishing a model school. However, the best way I can accomplish this feat is to let you as a group do it. Therefore, I have allocated $75,000 to be used by this group to produce this project. There are two constraints that must be religiously adhered to: (1) You must abide by federal and state laws in the use of these funds, and (2) you must use your principal and me as resource persons." I further delineated that I would not interfere with their decisions unless I felt that they did not do their homework well, and I would only do this to provide proper direction and guidance. I insisted that the group meet outside the school district so that its sessions would not be disturbed. At first the teachers did not trust me. However, as time went on and they received my numerous polite thank yous for their comments, trust began to seep into our relationship. What was the result of the teacher's efforts? It exceeded my expectations. They went after their task with professional and aggressive pursuit that any superintendent would be proud of. They hired experts in the field to come into the district and share their knowledge and expertise with them so that they would have a current base on which to make decisions. They kept copious notes and produced minutes of each meeting to keep everybody informed. They invited me to their meetings to hear my ideas and concerns and acted on them in one way or another. They produced a book that described all of their plans and activities and a time schedule. On two occasions I brought in substitute teachers so that the group would have time to complete its plans. Two secretaries were assigned to the group. Although the group was only obligated to meet and work during the hours teachers were required to be at school, most of the members remained into the wee hours of the next morning to complete their tasks. The psychology of ownership does this; people go beyond the call of duty when they are the owners of change.

On June 10, 1970, I included the following comment as part of the introduction to the Master Plan the teachers had created.

"The following Master Plan represents six months of cooperative activity by a group of teaching professionals. The plan is unique in many ways, as is the Planning Committee which created it. As Chief School Officer of Wyandanch Public Schools I clearly demonstrated my faith in the professional competence of members on the Planning Committee by waiving any voting or veto prerogatives which were mine. Although I and other members of my administrative staff were always available in an advisory or resource capacity, the Planning

Committee had full and direct responsibility for creating the Master Plan. This unique commitment to and reliance upon a group of teaching professionals to make the important decisions has borne immense dividends.

"The Master Plan is a fine example of what teachers can do when they are given the opportunity to work together in creative freedom. It is a clear indication, to those who questioned the premise, that a group of dedicated and well-trained professionals can successfully crystallize and synthesize their ideas, judgment, and experience in order to provide better educational programming for youngsters, without administrative interference."

How Ownership Can Be Established in Education

The psychology-of-ownership principle can work in a school organization if it is applied in a meaningful manner and supported by a strong commitment by the superintendent and his or her central administration team. I believe that the following steps are necessary in order to make maximum use of this principle:

- Divide all teachers into teams, either by grade or by subject. There should be no more than 11 teachers on a given team. Select teaching champions to become team leaders.

- Train teacher teams in a variety of appropriate subjects such as team building, self-management, conflict resolution, problem-solving, and consensus. Require that all teachers receive a minimum of 50 hours of training annually.

- Use the statement of philosophy and the vision of excellence developed in your district as a basis for mini-training seminars for teachers and other school people. The goal of the seminars should be to familiarize them with the district's definition of excellence and how values, beliefs, goals, objectives, and performance standards should be used to achieve excellence.

- Train school administrators to become support staff and sponsors of teams. This will require gaining their commitment and teaching them how to perform in their new role.

- Conduct a series of meetings with teachers on a weekly basis for the purpose of explaining their multiple roles and what is expected of them as individual and team self-managers. Role playing should be used to enhance the explanation.

- Allocate a budget to each team and grant the teams freedom to use it for educational purposes.

- Eliminate barriers that may conflict with the ownership principle, such as rigidly defined job descriptions, organizational charts, and inegalitarian practices.

- Recognize feats of excellence and provide immediate feedback no matter how small the act. All teams deserve to receive immediate feedback about how they are performing.

- Make indicated improvements in the program after retaining an outsider to come into the school district to evaluate the program.

Strategies for Achieving Excellence

- Establish an employee consultative committee and give it the responsibility for handling lateness, absenteeism, and other disciplinary matters.

- Look for practices that will help inculcate the psychology-of-ownership principle throughout the school organization, and implement them. Some of these are as follows:

— Avoid fixed or assigned authority

— Attain results through teamwork

— Encourage person-to-person communication

— Have objectives and performance standards set by those who must achieve them

— Have problems solved by those closest to them

— Organize tasks and functions on the basis of individual interests and commitments

— Give administrators sponsorship status (encourage them to become advocates in behalf of teachers and other school people)

— Decentralize authority

— Train people as generalists

- Organize a self-sufficient problem-solving team to perform a specific job. Give the team a list of the basic tasks involved and allocate a budget for the project. Tasks should include (1) selection of a champion to lead the team; (2) creation of a plan;

3) use of expert to clarify the plan; (4) presentation of the plan to central administrators; and (5) execution of the plan.

- Visit such best-run companies such as People Express, Dana Corporation, Quad/Graphics, W. L. Gore & Associates, and Kollmorgen to see how the psychology of ownership is operating. Upon returning to the school district, prepare a plan for emulating those principles and practices that are appropriate for your school district.

- Organize two separate teams, one made up of school administrators and the other made up of teachers. Fortify each team with information on the psychology-of-ownership principle and request that each team prepare a separate plan for giving teachers more ownership of their job. Duplicate copies of each plan for all team members. Arrange for both teams to meet outside the school district for a day to discuss similarities and dissimilarities of the two plans and reach a consensus on one plan. Implement the plan.

- Request that each teacher (and other school people too, for that matter) make a list of ways in which the principal gets in the way of teachers' performance. Combine the lists into one list. Give the list to the principal. Have him or her prepare an action plan to deal with the items on the list, or give a reason why a particular item cannot be changed.

- Permit school people to bid on a job that was formerly contracted out of the school district.

Achieve a Balance Between Loose and Tight Properties

The consensus from the voluminous material on management is that in order to manage well one must use both head and heart.
            —Jacquelyn Wonder and Priscilla Donovan

To attain excellence, school districts must control certain essential and important elements of the organization with rigid policies and procedures, while at the same time allowing school administrators and other school people great leeway in conducting the day-to-day affairs of the school district. With a proper balance of loose and tight properties, school districts will avoid the extremes of undue looseness and rigid controls and take one more step toward achieving excellence.

Tom Peters and Robert Waterman use the concept of loose vs. tight properties to describe the fact that although the best-run companies are rigidly controlled, they permit their people a great deal of freedom. Loose, or soft, properties encompass a variety of factors, such as extensive experimentation; campus-like work environment; flexible organizational structures; support for champions; positive feedback; tolerance of mistakes;

17

intimate social networks; autonomy for individuals, teams, and divisions; open door policies, etc. In all of these areas the best-run companies tend to be very people oriented, focusing on the positive and human side of management. At the same time, the best-run companies foster a set of tight properties that leave nothing to chance. Most are dominated by a company "culture"—a set of rigid shared values that focus on intense, frequent, and immediate feedback; concise reports; closeness to the customer; peer pressure; and intense review of performance by both supervisors and peers.

Loose-Tight Properties of the Best-Run Companies

The cultures of the best-run companies allow for the ambiguity between the loose and tight properties. At IBM, soft properties include respect for the individual, a no-lay-off policy, and an open-door policy. Some of the hard restrictions relate to not drinking on the job, adhering to sales quotas, and servicing the customer well. Over the years, this last property has been an overriding value at IBM. Everyone from the clerk to the chief executive officer is required to do whatever it takes to ensure that the customers are serviced well. Pity the person who does not embark on a path that is customer service oriented! Deviation from this hard and fast property is absolutely not tolerated at IBM.

At Hewlett-Packard, the manner in which things are done in the company is known as the HP way." Built into the HP way are loose and tight properties. For example, a key element in controls at Hewlett-Packard is management-by-objectives. However, the manner in which goals and objectives are mutually agreed upon and achieved varies to some degree, depending on the persons involved and the situation. If objectives are achieved on or above plan, a person's performance activities can be loose. On the other hand, if objectives are achieved below plan, tight and rigid controls are enforced in an effort to improve performance.

On the loose side, fluid movement within the company has always been 3M's hallmark. Top management considers the company's structure to be more biological than traditional. Whenever a new product generates a certain amount of sales, a new division is born. On the tight-side, promotion from within 3M is an absolute. Top-level managers particularly the chief executive officer, are virtually never hired from outside the company. Odetics, Inc. produces extremely sophisticated devices, such as space-borne tape recorders, time-lapse video recorders, and courtroom audio recorders. During a critical moment in the history of this company, it tightened reins on a group of its people by requiring that they work many long hours to get one of their recorders to pass an extremely important testing program. Once the machine passed the test, however, the company loosened its reins again—a band was hired to parade through the plant, and then free ice cream was given to the employees for a job well done.

One of Procter & Gamble's tight properties is that it promotes strictly from within and strictly by performance. The company is noted for researching a subject to death before it launches a new product. Thoroughness is an overriding hard value at Procter & Gamble. In addition, the one-page memorandum is a must for all managers. (It has been reported that one memo was rewritten 47 times before it was accepted by a supervisor!) On the other hand, people at Procter & Gamble are expected to make decisions on their own and are encouraged to use initiative and be creative and achievement oriented.

An interesting aspect of the loose-tight management approach is the way it resolves the apparent contradiction between freedom and coordination and cooperation. The best-run companies are simultaneously giving their people greater freedom and getting greater coordination and cooperation from them. Improved coordination and cooperation, which involve the mind, heart, and soul, can only occur among people who are free. For example, people at Apple Computer are organized into teams and are given a great deal of latitude in performing their jobs. As a result, Apple reached Fortune's 500 status faster than any other company in history.

There are numerous other stories similar to those cited above that verify that increased freedom brings improved coordination and cooperation among people and the pursuit of excellence. Freedom on the job has not always been important. However, with changing times and conditions, a greater number of people have been come to understand their own need for self- esteem and self-actualization through their work, and as a result, freedom has become more and more important. Soft, or loose, properties result only when people are given freedom. Controls are at the heart of hard, or tight, properties, and they are needed in order to increase the probability that the freedom given to people will result in the attainment of goals, objectives, and performance standards. An example of a company that has achieved an excellent balance is Advanced Micro Devices. On the soft side, this company gives its people freedom to create and innovate as well as the opportunity to share in the success of the enterprise through profit sharing. On the hard side, it publishes its financial goals so that all human efforts are concentrated in meeting them: compound annual sales growth in excess of 30 percent; return on capital greater than cost of capital; debt at no more than one third of total capital; after tax return on equity greater than 25 percent; and pretax operating margin on sales greater than 15 percent. The rules in excellent companies deal with quality, service, innovation, and experimentation. The rules in not-so-excellent companies deal with limiting, constraining, and controlling people. Excellent companies are both externally and internally focused: externally in that they are profoundly driven by their desire to provide service, quality, and innovative problem-solving in supporting their customers; internally in that their people are encouraged to control quality rather than to rely on a quality-control department.

External vs. Internal Contradiction

In public education, the external-versus-internal contradiction should have a special meaning. School organizations should be simultaneously externally focused and internally focused. They should be externally focused on providing quality education, competing academically with other schools (public as well as private), and seeking innovative programs and teaching methods to improve the education of students. On the other hand, school organizations should also be internally focused on organizing the school district people into multiple teams for the purpose of attaining improved results in all areas. Policies should be designed to permit teams to evaluate themselves as well as individual team members, encour-

21

age internal competition among school building teams and among schools, intensify communication, inculcate the school and classrooms with a family feeling, foster an open-door policy, give teachers and teams autonomy, and provide for more fluidity and flexibility. The internal focus should be on people.

Efficiency vs. Effectiveness Contradiction

One aspect of loose-tight properties that has implications for school districts is the efficiency vs. effectiveness contradiction. School administrators typically operate on the premise that in order to to achieve cost efficiency it is best to perform on a large scale—for example, by constructing a few large school buildings rather than several smaller ones. However, this has not been true for business and industry and probably is not true for public education. In the excellent companies, "small is beautiful" in almost all situations. This notion has two implications for school districts: School buildings, particularly high schools, should be constructed on a small scale, and school personnel should be organized into teams. These two policies will result in the most efficient use of space and school personnel. The smallness of space enhances motivation and improves communication and the quality of service. Decreased cost and greater efficiency will occur over the long run because of quality of service, productivity, innovativeness, result- sharing, consensus, participation, humanness, harmony, and a focus on internal problem-solving. Although the cost may be higher initially, once the "small is beautiful" concept is accepted, the system will be more cost-efficient and effective.

Smart-Dumb Rule

Peters and Waterman describe a contradiction which they refer to as the smart-dumb rule. In business and industry, the "smart" managers are the ones who design complicated incentive programs, produce elaborate strategic plans, and develop complicated evaluation instruments. They are, in essence, managers who may be too smart for their own good. They are also the managers who concentrate more on the structure and less on the process. On the other hand, the "dumb" managers, according to Peters and Waterman, don't understand why every product cannot be of the highest quality. They don't understand why the customer cannot get the best service. They are personally affronted when a product is defective. They don't understand why new and improved products cannot be created. They are the managers of the best-run companies in America who believe in people and what they are capable of doing—with the right kind of leadership.

In public education, the "smart" school administrators are the ones who design elaborate organizational charts and demand strict adherence to them. They produce scores of job descriptions and place them in large binders. They institute comprehensive management-by-objectives programs requiring the attainment of an unbelievable number of objectives. They seek gaps in the structure of the school organization and devise a sophisticated system for filling them.

The "dumb" school administrators are concerned with process as well as with structure. They don't understand why every kid can't learn, and they will strictly supervise and counsel those teachers whose kids are not achieving at an appropriate level. They are equally

23

interested in what happens during the performance evaluation and what took place before it. They are concerned about the rate of academic achievement among kids as well as the methods used to improve student learning and growth. They are incensed when they hear teachers call kids "stupid," "average," or dumb." On the other hand, they are concerned about maintaining a strict discipline code in their schools. They are concerned about the effects of teacher absenteeism on student performance and will develop appropriate instruments to track teachers absences and initiate appropriate actions. They believe that there is some good in every human being; it's just that some need more freedom and fewer controls and others need more control and less freedom. Finally, they believe that God did not make any imperfect kids or teachers, just different ones. The "dumb" school administrators are simplistic.

Steps in Adopting Loose-Tight Properties

What must school administrators do to adopt loose-tight properties? There are three steps:

First, develop an explicit statement of the values by which the school district operates. The establishment of loose-tight properties in public education is made difficult by the absence of a viable culture. Ambiguity in an organization can be of functional value only if a strong culture is exhibited through the inculcation of shared values. Most school districts have not taken the time to arrive at a set of beliefs that characterizes the school organization. There is no formalized set of unified beliefs or values system that holds the total school district together. Without shared values, there is no foundation for loose-tight properties.

Second, give detailed attention to key result areas of the school district; leave nothing to chance. Key result areas are those areas in which repercussions will occur if operations are not performed in a satisfactory or timely manner. These include budgetary controls, policies regarding performance expectations, long- and short-range planning activities, performance evaluation, and personnel recruitment and selection practices.

I am reminded of a new superintendent of schools of a medium-sized urban school district, who seemed oblivious to the school district's multi-million-dollar budget deficit. When I spoke to one of her assistants about developing a three- or five-year plan for reducing the budget, my advice went unheeded. The state department of education interceded and sent in its representative to monitor the fiscal affairs of the school district. In essence, because the superintendent failed to take a proactive stance on her budget problem, the intervention of the state department of education put her in a reactive mode and lessened her ability to lead.

There are several areas of the school district that must be governed by tight properties and given close scrutiny. The budget is one of these areas. One reason superintendents get into certain problems with the budget is that most of them are specialists. They tend to cater to their area of expertise and to leave to their assistants certain facets of school administration that should be governed by tight policies. A generalist is not likely to experience this problem because of his or her macroscopic view of the school system.

Once a strong culture is in place and areas requiring tight policies have been recognized and accommodated, the third step involves identifying those soft properties that loosen the reins on school people and enable them to become more productive. The soft properties I am referring to might include instituting an open-door policy, fostering a family climate, implementing egalitarian principles and practices, and providing more autonomy to school people.

In an effort to infuse these loose properties into the school district, administrators must plan training sessions to identify, discuss, and clarify each property statement. Following the sessions, all administrators and supervisors should be required to adhere religiously to the loose or soft properties that have been established.

A prevailing problem in public education is that far too many school districts are governed by either too many loose or too many tight properties instead of an equal balance of both. For example, in a high school that I spent about a month studying, I found an abundance of loose properties and too few tight properties. Teachers were never evaluated by the principal. There was only one meeting held between the teachers and principal during the school year. New teachers received very little constructive assistance from either the principal and or department chairperson. Time-on-task was not within minimum limits. There was virtually no training and development going on in the school. A number of teachers were having affairs with students. Drugs were being used by a few staff members and numerous students. The one tight property I was able to observe was the follow-up of student absenteeism, but this was due primarily to the fact that records of absenteeism were computerized.

On the other hand, an elementary school in the same school district had too few soft or loose properties. In fact, it was just the opposite of the high school. The principal had rules for everything, from how the bulletin boards were to be prepared to how the objectives in the plan book were to be written. Her style of management was strictly Theory X. She communicated to her teachers through a weekly newsletter (which contained numerous spelling errors, poor grammar and contradictions). In addition, she held frequent staff meetings, at which there was evidence of a hostile relationship between the principal and certain teachers who regarded themselves as professionals. During the performance evaluation process, when a principal is expected to probe and get teachers to identify strengths and weaknesses in their teaching, this principal acted more like a warden of a prison, telling the teachers what they did improperly during the observation. Obviously, the hostile relationship between the principal and members of her staff continued throughout these sessions. Because of the excessively tight properties, the atmosphere in the school was so negative that it had a negative impact on student academic achievement, and on the teachers' absentee rate which was 12 percent, more than three times the national average.

A critical review of both properties reveals that soft properties tend to be people oriented; they represent the manner in which school administrators should be expected to treat their people. On the other hand, the hard properties apply to the manner in which jobs should be done. When there is an equal balance between the loose and tight properties, the path to excellence should proceed without many problems. However, most school administrators have not been trained to understand the loose-tight properties concept, and therefore have not made a conscious effort to assess the degree to which there is a balance between the two properties.

Strategies for Achieving Excellence

- Identify those hard/tight properties (involving strategy, systems, and structure) that are absolutely necessary to achieve excellence. Then identify those soft/loose properties (involving style, skills, staff, superordinate goals) that are also absolutely necessary to achieve excellence.

- Check your statement of philosophy to determine whether this document truly reflects those hard and soft properties you have identified as being important to the success of your school district.

- Develop a training and development program consisting of 15- to 20-minute sessions to infuse certain soft and hard properties in your school district.

- Prepare a questionnaire to assess the attitudes of high school students toward the soft and hard properties of the school district. When the results have been tabulated, present the information to the students and request that they describe what steps should be taken to reach an equal balance.

- Discontinue, just for one occasion, the present method of assessing the performance of teachers and school administrators, and instead design and use an instrument that will highlight the hard and soft properties used by individual teachers and administrators. How does the result compare with expectations? What should be done to reach an equal balance?

Become More Egalitarian

Participation means that managers must learn to
share power rather than try to accumulate it. It calls
for deeper insights and broader understanding of
human needs than many managers have acquired in
learning how to manage the old way.

—Perry Pascarella

Many of the best-run companies, through their humanistic and egalitarian principles, make it possible for
people to graduate to a point where they are motivated
by self-actualization rather than by a lower-level need.
When conditions within the organization allow employees to become self-actualized, the resulting synergistic
work environment aids the company in pursuing excellence.

An important component of the best-run company is
people whose main goal is not the not self-serving one of
providing a living for themselves, but rather that of
promoting the organization and its purposes. Cooperation replaces competition; teamwork, replaces individual
effort; love, replaces hate; harmony replaces discord; and
higher-level goals replace lower- level goals. To some
extent, working life and family life merge in a social-
economic life that benefits the individual, the organization, and the community. The main thrust of the best-
run company is directed toward creating a situation in

which the individual and the organization help each other.

When employees enjoy full participation in a company and share in the earned rewards, they become complete, and respected individuals, thus lead a more meaningful existence. An organization that really respects its people will allow them to work not as underlings answering to a higher authority, but as human beings working together as equals for a common cause. Those who formulated the American Declaration of Independence stated this principle better than I could when they said: "All men are created equal and are endowed by their Creator with certain inalienable rights."

Definition of Egalitarianism

As used in business and industry the term *egalitarianism* refers to the belief that all human beings should have equal economic, social, and political rights to fulfill their basic needs on the job. *Economic rights* pertain to the equal opportunity that all human beings should have to maintain a job in consonance with their personal characteristics and intelligence in order to obtain food, clothing, shelter, and other amenities. *Social rights* refer to the equal opportunity that all human beings should have to participate in groups and to engage in social and recreational activities. In the context of the job, *political rights* refer to the equal opportunity that individuals should have to assist in the operation of the company through decision making and problem solving—in effect, opportunities to influence decisions that will affect them.

The *Oxford English Dictionary*'s definition of egalitarianism contains three conditions: (1) having equal dignity, rank, or privileges with others; (2) being equal in power, ability, achievement, or excellence; and (3) being fair, impartial, equal, or in proportion. The first of these definitions of egalitarianism identifies and describes the three essential areas covered by this concept. The subsequent describes the implications of rights in these areas.

Evaluating Egalitarianism

There are, numerous ways to evaluate whether treatment is or is not egalitarian, and any such decision is open to question. However, the following are general rules for determining whether or not a particular act, benefit, or burden is egalitarian.

1. Consider the rule of distribution. The *rule of distribution* maintains that in a purely egalitarian organization, benefits and burdens are divided equally among all people.

When management at the Mellon-Stuart Company initiated its employee-ownership program, it was decided that shares in the company would be sold only to a few top managers. Because not all employees were allowed to purchase shares of the company's stock, this decision by management was not an egalitarian one. No doubt management had some logical reasons for its actions. However, denying a benefit to a group implies that one group of individuals is superior to another. In a purely egalitarian culture, all individuals are treated equally. (I am elated to announce that during the 1980s Mellon modified its employee- ownership plan to include all of its 450 employees.)

2. Consider the rule of equalization. The *rule of equalization* rests on the principle that all people should have the same rights, privileges, rank, status, and power. Usually the rule of equalization pertains to "perks" that are given to management to enhance their image and status. Although it is natural to want to enhance the status of one group of employees, this should not be done at the expense of another group. Traditional terms that have been used over the years, such as "boss," "superior," or "master," tend to reflect an inegalitarian image. Titles are not the only element used to elevate the status or to polish the image of management. Other status- and image-improvement perks include large and well-located offices, private secretaries, chauffeured limousines, company jets, company hotel suites, executive dining rooms, private dining clubs, and reserved parking places.

In an effort to abide by the rule of equalization, companies have adopted a number of innovative practices. For example, at W. L. Gore & Associates, the term "sponsor" is used instead of "boss;" People Express refers to all employees as "managers;" at the IBM Research Center in Yorktown Heights, New York, the rule of equalization has guided the construction of an office building in which all offices are exactly the same size and are furnished in exactly the same manner. At Apple Computers all managers are expected to type their own letters and answer their own phones. No longer do many companies provide their managers with a chauffeured limousine, as ITT did for Harold Geneen when he was chief executive officer of ITT.

3. Consider the rule of relevance. The *rule of relevance* states that inequality of treatment may actually be egalitarian if the benefit or burden is *major* and there

is a *logical* reason for the difference. Before we can say that a policy or an act is inegalitarian, we must examine it to determine whether the benefit (to the company) or burden (to the group) is of significant magnitude and whether there is a sound reason for the selective application of the policy to a certain group. When major differences and sound reasons for them are obvious, ostensibly egalitarian treatment may actually be inegalitarian. For example, the Japanese people were not actually being egalitarian when they ignored the *relevance provisions* of equalitarianism by ignoring inequality of duties and length of employment when setting employee wages. To justify this form of inegalitarianism, the term *psychological egalitarianism* was developed, referring to the belief that, since wages are needed for employees to satisfy basic human needs, they should be distributed on an *equal* basis regardless of differences in duties and responsibilities.

A word of caution: Human beings have a tendency to believe what they want to believe, regardless of the facts. Therefore, unless major differences and sound reasons for them can clearly be shown, treatment should be declared to be inegalitarian. Because applying the rule of relevance can be very subjective, it is likely to cause a great deal of anxiety. An effective way to determine whether or not an act is egalitarian is to establish a committee composed of a cross section of employees and charge it with the responsibility of determining when a benefit or burden is egalitarian. The mode of decision making might be either majority or consensus. This committee might be established when a particular principle or practice is being considered for adoption or when a company's policy is being evaluated.

Common Inequalities

Inequalities have always existed in organizations. Some experts believe that ending inegalitarianism in one area will have a residual effect on other areas. However, this has not proven the case. The following is a list of inequalities that exist to some extent in almost all organizations.

Inequality in Status. When material or economic conditions have reached a certain point, employees turn their attention to social and self-esteem needs. Therefore, the conscientious egalitarian manager will direct his or her attention to reducing or eliminating wide disparities in status. For example, at Wal-Mart Company everyone is identified as an "associate;" Disney describes its employees as "cast members"; Trammell Crow Company refers to all of its employees as "partners"; and Northwestern Mutual Life refers to the company as the "family." Many American organizations tend to ignore the fact that such a small move as reducing the number of titles could enhance their employees' self-esteem within the organization.

Inequality in the Distribution of Influence. Another form of nonmaterial inequality is inequality in the distribution of influence. Although a large number of organizations have unions and many also have laborers who are well educated and have a high standard of living, distribution of influence has improved only to a small extent. Influence within companies remains in the hands of a relatively small, privileged group of people called top management. Even though many organizations maintain that they have a democratic form of management, critical review of their management style reveals it to be authoritative. A few egalitarian companies are making progress in reducing the inequalities in the distribution of influence by insisting that decisions be arrived at by consensus and by permitting employees to become owners of the company.

Inequality in Job Satisfaction. Another form of inequality lies in the differing opportunities available to employees for obtaining job satisfaction. These differences may relate to length of holidays, sick-day allowances, pensions, incentives, reserved parking spaces, use of a company car, and other perks that are given to some managers but not to most employees. However, the most striking differences in benefits usually involve very substantial tax-free benefits, such as housing, bonuses, profit-sharing, and large awards made upon retirement.

Inequalities in Work Environment. Inequality in the conditions under which employees work seems to be prevalent in many organizations. While many managers have palatial offices, glamorous secretaries, and wall-to-wall carpeting, nonmanagement employees usually have none of these luxuries. The inequalities cited above reflect the old adage "Rank has its privilege." However, companies are beginning to realize they can no longer bestow large benefits upon their managers without considering their other employees—at least not if they expect all employees to produce in an exceptional manner. Today's organizations must nurture individual self-respect among their employees. One of the most effective ways of doing this is by reducing the number of inequalities that exist in the organization, continuing only those that can be soundly justified.

Justification for Egalitarianism

Justifications for egalitarianism tend to be all- encompassing, providing almost spiritual parameters for dealing with employees. Some of these justifications are as follows:

- Egalitarianism *is* the normative baseline for all human behavior. Therefore, any inegalitarianism must be supported on solid grounds.

- Egalitarianism brings with it increased respect and concern for larger numbers of people.

- The infusion of egalitarianism reduces dissension and disorder and increases harmony and respect among employees and managers.

- Egalitarianism is a healthy state of mind that enhances the achievement of individual and organizational goals.

- Egalitarianism is intrinsically more desirable and morally right than other forms of treatment.

When organizations create a feeling of egalitarianism in the work environment, employees feel less threatened. This is because rank, status, power, and prestige are threatening to many people, particularly if they are used as tools to impress or intimidate others. Any respect that is generated is quite mixed with envy, resentment, and fear. People have a tendency to trust those who are their equals because they believe that they can have more influence on their behavior and attitudes. Power, on the other hand, distorts and reduces that influence. Consider two managers—George Jenkins, an egalitarian who was the chief executive officer of Publix Super Markets, and Harold Geneen, an inegalitarian who was formerly the chief executive officer of ITT. Both of these managers were successful. Jenkins's management style was described as subtle and people-oriented. People enjoyed working for him because they felt that he and his managers respected them. Much of his effectiveness resulted from the sense that employees felt that they were equals of Jenkins—that he influenced them and they influenced him. Even though George Jenkins no longer serves as Publix chief executive officer, this influencing force still exists in the company and the company's net sales and profits are still increasing on a yearly basis.

On the other hand, Geneen's management style has been characterized as ruthless, punitive, tension-ridden, and devoid of concern for the humanity of his employees. People worked for Geneen because they feared him. He influenced people, and under his management, ITT made remarkable gains. However, whereas Jenkins influenced people through referrent power (respected leadership), Geneen exerted influence through coercive power. Thus, when Geneen left ITT, any influence he had wielded over the people he left behind had little propelling effect on the growth of the company. A review of the annual growth record of ITT after the Geneen era reveals that the company has remained virtually at a standstill.

Why was Jenkins more successful than Geneen in establishing a pattern of growth that continued after he left the company? Because of Jenkin's sensitivity to people, he infused a people-oriented philosophy into the entire organization. Organizational creativity was a natural outcome of a strong people-oriented culture, a comprehensive succession plan, and a rigid policy of promotion from within. Because Geneen was primarily concerned about the bottom line, he did not foster a strong people-oriented culture. He did not institute a succession plan, nor did he promote someone from within as his successor.

Egalitarian Principles

There are six egalitarian principles that should be observed in the management of people.

1. Equality of Treatment.

Despite differences in characteristics, traits, and intelligence, all human beings are entitled to equal treatment in terms of respect and concern. Egalitarian companies demonstrate in a number of ways their intention to treat their employees as equals. For example:

- At Armstrong World Industries, everyone from the president to factory line worker, eats in the same company cafeteria.

- At Borg-Warner, there are no reserved parking spaces for managers. Everyone, including the chief executive officer, must fend for himself or herself in seeking parking space.

- In the headquarters of CRS Sirrene, Inc., there are no enclosed offices. Even top level managers work in "action stations" separated by shoulder-high partitions. People are regularly rotated from one building to another and from one work station to another.

- When Delta's flight schedules were sharply curtailed in 1973 during the oil embargo, the company did not lay off a single person. Instead, 600 pilots and stewardesses were reassigned to such jobs as loading cargo, cleaning airplanes, selling tickets, and making reservations.

- At Donnelly, everyone is expected to keep his or her own records and is responsible to other team members. Each team is linked to other teams through team leaders.

- At E. I. Dupont, all employees and retirees have received free medical examinations since 1916.

2. Equality in Satisfying Basic Needs.

All people should be entitled to use their physical and intellectual endowment to satisfy their basic needs.

This principle is extremely important, because it promotes satisfaction not only of economic needs but also of safety, social, self-esteem, and self-actualization needs. These needs set parameters for management to follow in establishing a work environment. The philosophy of the company, the management style of the staff, and the quality of the total work environment should reflect the accommodation of these basic needs.

Dana Corporation helps satisfy its employees' needs by permitting them to own a part of the company, by recognizing them for superior performance, and by providing them with the freedom to participate in setting their own goals and evaluating their own performance. Celestial Seasonings helps its people to satisfy their basic needs by identifying, cultivating, training, retraining, and rewarding those who are committed to moving the company forward. Hewlett-Packard helps its employees to satisfy their basic human needs by emphasizing working together, sharing responsibilities, and rewarding outstanding contributions to company goals.

3. Equality in Finding Meaningful Work.

All people should be provided the opportunity to find meaning in their work. This principle supports the basic need of self- actualization; that is, opportunities should be afforded to everybody on the job, regardless of position, to find jobs suited for them and to become all that they can be, within the limits of their abilities, and talents.

Jack Warosh of 3M was a packaging systems salesman when he was offered a promotion to sales manager in a different part of the country. He turned down the promotion. Today, he is still a salesman; however, he did accept an additional assignment as a field sales trainer. Jack feels that these two responsibilities best fit his interests and qualifications, and 3M is content to allow him to make that decision. John Wetz is a technical specialist at 3M responsible for a statistical consulting in the company's division of Information Systems and Data Processing. The wide scope of his job allows him to solve a wide variety of corporate problems in such departments as Manufacturing, Legal, Sales, and Marketing. 3M encourages all of its employees to find their own career paths; as a result, they control their own destiny with respect to finding meaningful work. At Nissan Motor Manufacturing Corporation, U.S.A., the more varied jobs a person performs in his or her area of responsibility, the more money he or she makes. The company pays employees for taking advantage of training and development opportunities. Obviously, those who have acquired the appropriate training and who have performed well on the job are the ones who are eventually promoted. Dana Corporation maintains that it has "an obligation to provide training and the opportunity for development to our productive people who want to improve their skills, expand their career opportunities or simply further their general education." At Digital Equipment Corporation, newly hired employees are not automatically slotted in a specific position.

4. Equality of Opportunity.

All people should have the opportunity to apply for any position, regardless of level, on an equal and competitive basis, regardless of differences in social status, economic resources, personal characteristics, and intelligence.

This principle, supported by federal and state legislation, guarantees each employee the opportunity to compete for any position in the organization. The principle is based on the premise that if everyone has an equal start, each person should attain a position that reflects his or her abilities and other resources. The French Declaration of the Rights of Man summarizes this principle by proclaiming that all human beings "are equally eligible for all honors, places, and employment, according to their different abilities; without any other distinction than that of their virtues and talents."

For years, minorities, women, and the handicapped have been denied equal opportunity on the job. Recently a number of egalitarian companies have been leaders in equalizing opportunities for those who have been forsaken for so many years. John G. Smale, President and chief executive officer of Procter & Gamble, has this to say about what his company is doing about equality of opportunity: "I want to emphasize that there is nothing inconsistent in the selectivity of our hiring process and our declaration to equal employment. . . . We look particularly hard for minority talent . . . in fields of interest to our company that attract fewer minorities and women; we seek to enlarge the pool of qualified individuals available for employment with scholarship and fellowship programs. . . . For example, because minorities and women are under represented in the nation's engineering schools, Procter & Gamble sponsors a scholarship program to encourage the enrollment in engineering schools. Procter & Gamble contributes to two programs designed to stimulate minority enrollment in the nation's leading graduate schools of management. Our research and development and engineering divisions also provide financial support for minorities in specific disciplines of interest to those divisions."

At the end of 1983, IBM had approximately 3600 women, 3000 minority managers, and several thousand handicapped employees. IBM expanded its program to support minority-owned business in the United States by doing more than $90 million worth of business with minority-owned firms, purchasing more than $50 million worth of products and services from companies owned primarily by women, and buying more than $16 million worth of products and services from companies that employ large numbers of handicapped people.

At 3M, women and minorities accounted for only 6.3 percent of the professional employees in 1982, and more than 22 percent in 1984. In 1982, women and minorities constituted 2 percent of 3M's managers and supervisors; by 1984 they constituted more than 10 percent. In 1972, women and minorities made up 3.9 percent of 3M's industrial sales force; by 1984 they composed more than 20 percent. Lewis W. Lehr, chairman of 3M, says, "We have women who are engineers in our factories. We have women working on the lines. . . . We have women salespeople, women in our public relations area, and lots of women scientists. We have women in our central area, our financial area, everywhere there is an interest and an available job, we have women—and other minorities. . . . We have an executive conference which consists of about the top division management level people, and we have two women in that now."

5. *Equality in Distribution.*

Within the limits of the rule of relevance, every person should have an equal share of benefits or burdens. This important operating principle should provide the foundation for the distribution of income and fringe benefits.

W. L. Gore & Associates, Inc. has established an egalitarian way of sharing its profits with employees who are referred to as "associates." The company attempts to balance its compensation pay so that excess profits are accumulated from time to time. The excess is distributed to associates in proportion to their historical contribution; that is a portion of the excess profit is distributed in proportion to one's previous three-year total compensation, and the remainder in proportion to one's current compensation. The egalitarian aspect of this practice rests in the proportioning of the two sums and in the choice of time periods. The basic premise is that compensation paid is proportional to contributions made, and that a large proportion of a current financial excess is a consequence of efforts made in previous years of service.

6. *Equality of Power.*

Every person should be provided with opportunities to share power with those in positions of authority. This principle is based on the belief that each person has something to offer to the organization. Those in positions of authority should look for and make opportunities to share power with their employees. Eliminating titles, levels, and symbols is one way of equalizing power between managers and employees. Another way is to have employees make decisions that were hitherto reserved for managers.

At Nissan Corporation, management shares power with employees by giving them opportunities to solve job-related problems through an "involvement circle" program which operates in the administrative offices as well as on the plant floor. The involvement circles are similar to Japanese quality control circles; groups of employees meet regularly on company time to solve problems dealing with safety, quality, and/or productivity.

Procter & Gamble maintains that management should share power with employees by making the entire organization conducive to the involvement and participation of employees in the daily conduct of the business. The company stipulates that management must always be open to new ideas and better ways of doing business and keep in mind that people change as society changes, that they acquire new attitudes about work itself, that they develop new aspirations, and that they change in their expectations of the nature of the work.

Problems in Interpreting Egalitarianism

Egalitarianism is not an easy concept to grasp. It is by nature subjective, and the different values of the various parties tend to contribute to their misinterpretation of the real intent of the egalitarian principles.

The following is a list of problems that may arise in the interpretation of egalitarian principles.

1. Managers may not understand the inherent advantages and benefits of sharing and equalizing power with employees. Managers should realize that sharing their power with employees is not abolishing it but rather making better use of it to get things done.

2. All egalitarian and inegalitarian principles must be qualified, because they are not absolutes. The fact that the interpretation of the substance of each principle is up to the individual or the group may cause difficulties.

3. Political equality entails allowing all employees to influence decisions regarding the operations of the organization; however, a particular decision arrived at through consensus may result in inegalitarian treatment. For example, a management-employee team might reach a majority decision to provide a certain fringe benefit exclusively for managers merely because they are managers, i.e., treatment that cannot be supported by the rule of relevance.

A generally effective method for preventing the emergence of inegalitarian practices is to ensure that all groups that will be affected by a decision are equally represented in the decision-making process.

4. Implementation of egalitarian principles may stifle creativity, individuality, and diversity. Although this is seldom a problem, it can become one if managers do not follow through on the rule of relevance and provide

45

incentives for outstanding (major difference) performance by individuals, teams, and divisions, using recognition, awards and other relevant methods.

5. After the distinction between egalitarianism and inegalitarianism has been defined and organizational goals have been clarified, the adoption of one or the other policy is a matter of supportive judgment. Because egalitarianism is a humanistic process for the treatment of people, it maybe difficult to sustain objective criteria.

6. Greater equality of opportunity may generate frustration and unhappiness because of the competitiveness it engenders. The company must try to see that employees compete in areas where they will achieve a degree of success. In a purely egalitarian company, a career path program is used as a basis for mapping out with employees a training-and-development program with employees to enhance their individual abilities in competing for positions with people inside and outside the company. In most of the more egalitarian organizations, a comprehensive training-and-development program dovetails with a personalized career path program for each employee. When such a program is coupled with a strong commitment by management to promote from within, there is no need for employees to fear the opportunity being afforded them to move up in the company. Opportunities in an egalitarian organization are limited only by the talents, skills, commitment, and ambition of each employee.

Egalitarianism Produces Results

When people feel good about themselves, they sense that other people feel good about them; when they feel good about others, the organization has taken one more step toward achieving excellence. The principles of egalitarianism help to create humanistic environment that improves people's self-esteem and thus has a positive effect on the tone of the organization. Hayes Associates, a consulting firm, studied nearly a half a million employees from various companies over a period of years. Their research findings indicate that egalitarian organizations are more productive than inegalitarian ones. I suspect this would be true for school districts also. Following is a summary of the conclusions of the Hayes study:

- Managers in egalitarian companies tend to reinforce a culture that emphasizes high quality.

- Egalitarian companies tend to seek people who value challenge and growth.

- People in egalitarian companies tend to believe that they are the company's most important asset.

- Credibility of information in egalitarian companies tends to be higher than in inegalitarian ones.

- Egalitarian companies tend to place less value on individual initiative and greater value on performance clarity.

- Egalitarian companies tend to place greater value on human resource development than do inegalitarian organizations.

- In egalitarian companies people's attitudes and self-confidence tend to be better and to improve with tenure.

- High-achieving companies tend to foster a more egalitarian culture than do low-achieving companies.

- People in egalitarian companies tend to be more satisfied with benefits than do those in inegalitarian companies.

- Women are more likely to leave inegalitarian companies than are men.

- Management is more in touch with its people in egalitarian companies than in inegalitarian companies.

- People in egalitarian companies are more concerned with challenge and learning whereas people in inegalitarian companies are more concerned with security and authority.

- Egalitarian companies tend to permit some duplication of efforts, which can lead to creative innovations.

- Egalitarian companies tend to share information more fully with employees.

Egalitarian Practices of the Best Companies

The economic principles and practices adopted by egalitarian companies are designed to make people feel that they can become much more than they are, and to remove barriers that restrict performance results.

Few companies can match the economic egalitarian

practices of Time, Inc. The company pays the entire cost of a dental plan for employees and their families. If an individual works beyond 8 p.m., the company gives him or her a stipend toward dinner and pays the entire cost of taking a taxi home. Through the company's profit-sharing plan, each person receives toward his or her account an amount equal to 10 percent of his salary. Employee pensions are completely paid by the company. An individual can use 3 to 10 percent of his or her salary to purchase company stock, Time will add 50 cents to each dollar used for that purpose. Time will also pay 100 percent of tuition for education in job-related fields, and 75 percent of tuition for studies that are not job related.

A number of companies offer employees "flex-time." Rolm Corporation takes the program one step further and offers its employees "flex-flex time," which means that employees can come to work whenever they want to, subject to the approval of their immediate supervisor or team. Any person who has worked more than six years at Rolm can take three months off at full pay, and some people have opted to take six weeks off at double pay. Moog, Inc. has an assortment of egalitarian economic practices, such as a family security package, above-average pay rates, 100 percent educational assistance, profit-sharing, job security, overtime equalization, employee handbook policy guidelines, personal time, and an extended vacation plan.

The egalitarian social principles and practices of the best-run companies vary. Moog has adopted more egalitarian social practices than many companies. It has no time clocks, no schedule breaks (employees can take a coffee break whenever they need one), and no bells or whistles.

H. B. Fuller Company's egalitarian social practices all extend outside of the company. The company encourages employees to participate in community affairs. Each year the company gives an Outstanding Volunteer Award to the one person who has done the most in terms of volunteering his or her time and energy for the community. At Christmas, the company's people collect toys and food and contribute them to the poor and needy. H. B. Fuller has established a local community affairs council which distributes a share of the funds that the company has allocated for charitable agencies in the community. The company also has a Rape and Sexual Assault Legal Advocate Program which has received attention for its excellence.

The best-run companies practice political egalitarianism by giving employees a voice in the decision-making process. At Donnelly Mirrors, employees are organized into teams. Each team sets its own production objectives based on the company's goals. Objectives are also set by individuals and vary from person to person. Doyle Dane Bernbach allows its people to decide whether they prefer to work on liquor or candy accounts. Whereas in most large companies there are as many as twelve levels, Nucor Corporation has no more than three levels separating production line people and the president of the company, in order to facilitate the decision-making process.

In most of the best-run companies there is an overriding value statement—a statement of the highest-ranked value of the company—which I usually refer to as the "sublimity statement." This statement, can be used to identify the type of culture the company desires. Sometimes the statement delineates an all-encompassing company style. Hewlett-Packard calls it the "HP way;" Delta calls it the "family spirit." At IBM it is "customer service." Other times the focus is somewhat narrower. At Publix Super Markets, it is "pleasing the customer." With Quad/Graphics, it is "helping people become something more than they every hoped to be." Worthington Industries, Inc.'s overriding value has a religious ring: "We treat our customers, employees, investors, and suppliers as we would like to be treated." Fairness, freedom, commitment, and discretion are the important values guiding the actions of the people at W. L. Gore & Associates. The founders at Procter & Gamble established the base and set the tone for the company by adopting as the sublimity value "find and hire good people. . . ."

Because people are trusted and respected in an egalitarian company, less formalized rules are used to control them. In many companies, there are no organizational charts, no job descriptions, no written rules to which people must strictly adhere, no time clocks, no dress codes, and nothing to separate one teammate from another, except what he or she does at a given time. Quite often, comments such as the following are heard in the best-run companies, substantiating the effectiveness of loose rules.

- "People tend to be more reliable than they were under strict rules and regulations."

- "We don't have any rules here. We are required to do what needs to be done."

- "People are given a lot of responsibility throughout all levels of our organization."

- "Because people are trusted here, few rules are needed."

An egalitarian culture seems to perpetuate a philosophy of self-management. People appreciate the freedom afforded them by management—the fact that, for example, if they have a good reason for breaking a unwritten or written rule, their action will be sanctioned by management. This trust permeates the company and provides some benefits that are not characteristic of inegalitarian companies.

In some of the best-run companies, people are referred to as a "family" or "extended family" in order to demonstrate the concern the organization has for the economic and social welfare of its people. The word "family" conveys the philosophical posture of the company and broadly describes how employees are respected and treated.

As an extension of employees' families, an egalitarian company is very much involved in economic and social welfare. Leo Burnett Company has one of the most unique sick-leave policies in the country. All employees with two or more years of service, receive full salary whenever they are stricken with a serious illness. When an individual of the Leo Burnett Company was scheduled to go to the hospital, the chief executive officer sent a company auto to transport her. And when a lifetime employee of Burnett died of a heart attack, a company representative went to the home of the widow to inform her that the company would take care of the college expenses of the children.

More and more of the best-run companies are beginning to subsidize early childhood services for their people. Workplace child care is of particular significance for one-parent families, not only because it is provided at a convenient location and at reduced costs, but also because it ensures them of child care that fits their employment schedule.

The family spirit in egalitarian companies always starts at the top with the behavior and attitude of the chief executive officer, who acts as a role model, for other top level and middle managers. At Armstrong World Industries, everyone including the president is on a first-name basis. This is how the president encourages both managers and employees to develop a family-like feeling throughout the company. At the Borg-Warner Corporation, the chief executive officer stresses the values of the Borg- Warner family through togetherness, open communication, respect, caring and teamwork.

Whereas many traditional companies have policies against hiring husband and wife teams, a few egalitarian companies are hiring them, and some permit them to travel together to training programs. When an employee is required to travel some distance from the employment site, some companies pay travel and living expenses of the spouses also. In an effort to give spouses a sense of the company culture, a few companies invite employees' spouses to attend orientation meetings. Another practice, that seems to be increasing in the best-run companies is arranging vacation trips for employees and their families. These trips may or may not include business sessions.

In many of the best-run companies, every birthday is recognized. Recognition of individual birthdays sometimes comes from the chief executive officer, who may maintain a computerized record of all company people and send either a card or letter. In some companies a supervisor will arrange to join with members of the person's family to give a birthday party. Sometimes, the company will reward the person with a birthday stipend.

Birthdays are not the only special event used by the best- run companies to recognize their people. Gifts are usually given to individuals on certain holidays—a turkey on Thanksgiving and food or a special gift on Christmas. It is not unusual for a company to share good news with its people (awarding of a contract, exceeding of a major goal, etc.) and to celebrate the event with a gift or a lavish party.

Most companies provide a variety of awards for people who exceed performance requirements. Gifts of paid vacations, radios, calculators, or computers are only a few of the ways companies recognize their people. In some companies, when goals are met, employees are allowed to buy stock at discounts. Leo Burnett Company goes to great lengths to establish special theme days and to bestow valuable gifts on all of its people. In many of the best-run companies, gifts and bonuses are presented to employees on the yearly anniversary of the founding of the company. Some managers have been known to serve breakfast or lunch to their employees on special occasions. At Celestial Seasonings, after an individual has been with the company three months, he or she receives a company T-shirt. Each person gets a check of $25 on his or her birthday. At Thanksgiving, everyone gets a check for $50, and at Christmas, a check for $100. Citicorp has a policy of recognizing up-and-coming managers by posting their names and biographies on a board called "Corporate Property," located in a room where only top-level managers are permitted.

The caring attitudes that permeate many of the best-run companies are demonstrated in their are attentiveness to the health and welfare of their employees.

Baxter Travenol Laboratories, Inc. constructed its own physical fitness facility, which is used by nearly 1000 employees to keep in shape. At E. I. Du Pont, safety slogans are posted throughout the company, free medical examinations are given to all workers including those who have retired, and numerous studies are made to determine the effects of various chemicals to which the people are exposed. Eastman Kodak Company is another organization that is serious about the health and welfare of its people. It maintains a staff of 275 people who provide free medical examinations to employees. Hewlett-Packard has ten different recreation areas to accommodate the health and social needs of its employees and their families. Johnson & Johnson has one of the country's finest health and welfare facilities. It consists of a large fitness center where employees can receive a physical examination and participate in a physical fitness program under the guidance of professionals. Such a program may involve losing weight, building and toning muscles, or engaging in other health-related activities. The physical fitness program of the Nissan Corporation extends throughout the company; fitness equipment is located at sites convenient for employees, who can use it during lunch time or breaks.

Some employees have shown their appreciation of humanistic nature of the best-run companies and the manner in which managers trust them. At Apple Computer, employees cheer and applaud every time one of their managers is introduced at the annual stockholders meeting and sales figures are reported. Delta Air Lines employees pledged nearly $1000 each to purchase a $30 million Boeing 767 jet for the company. In 1980, during the company's fiftieth anniversary, employees of Publix Super Markets presented its founder, George Jenkins, with a bronze medallion and a plaque with the inscription "To 'Mr. Publix' George W. Jenkins, the head of our Publix family. In appreciation of all the things you have done for us throughout the years." In 1985, employees at Worthington Industries bought double-page ads in the *Columbus Ohio Dispatch* and the *Columbus Citizen Journal* to congratulate John McDonnell, who had been the company's chief executive officer for twenty-five years. The ads said: "From the Employees at Worthington Industries, where the American free-enterprise system is at work; Mr. McDonnell, your efforts have improved our lives, families, and community." A secretary of Hewitt Associates, after seeing a notice in a local newspaper about some researchers who were investigating the 100 best companies, suggested, unbeknownst to the manager, that the researchers investigate Hewitt Associates. As a result, Hewitt Associates was compared with the other 100 best companies and ranked as a "superior" company for which to work, one of the ten best-paying companies, and one of the ten best companies for benefits.

Three Steps Toward Egalitarianism

In the quest for excellence, there are three steps a school district should take to begin working toward becoming more egalitarian. First, it should survey the human needs of all school people to determine which ones are being met and which ones are not. The survey form should contain a description of each need and a request that school people indicate what the school district can do to help them better fulfill each particular need. The following are examples of items you may want to include.

56

- Economic needs
  Every human being desires to work to satisfy his or her needs for food, shelter, clothing, and an occasional amenity. Think of your job. Are all of your economic needs being adequately fulfilled? Please indicate what the school district can do to help fulfill your economic needs.

- Security needs
  When human beings work to satisfy their economic needs, they want to do so within a safe environment, one that is free from physical danger and psychological stress. Please indicate what the school district can do to fulfill your security needs.

- Social needs
  In addition to economic and security needs, all human beings have a need to like and be liked by others, and to love and be loved by others. Please indicate ways in which the school district can help fulfill your social needs.

- Self-esteem needs
  All human beings also have a need to have a high opinion of themselves, and to be respected by and respectful of others. Please describe ways in which the school district can help fulfill your self-esteem needs.

- Actualization needs
  Even though human beings may be satisfying all of their other needs, they still have a need to become fully what they are capable of becoming. Please

describe what the school district can do to fulfill your self-actualization needs.

- Knowledge needs
  All human beings have a thirst for knowledge and information on and off the job. Do you get the knowledge and information you want? Please describe how the school district can help fulfill your need for knowledge.

The second step in working to create a more egalitarian school district is to analyze the completed survey forms. After determining common areas of agreement, interview a good cross section of school people to clarify common needs. For each identified need, identify policies, procedures, and activities that will help fulfill the needs. Once this step has been completed, study each need carefully and determine constraints and feasibility. Determine a cost factor for each need. At this time it may be necessary to modify a policy, procedure, or activity because the cost is too high. When your need- fulfillment plan has been completed, think of it as a three-year long-range plan. Obtain approval from the board of education to adopt the three-year need-fulfillment plan, making modifications and adjustment as necessary.

The third step is to hold a meeting to present the three-year plan to all school people, with back-up sessions given by the immediate supervisors. In some cases, the policies, procedures, and activities can be initiated without training administrators and supervisors; in other cases administrators and supervisors will have to be trained to implement the principles and practices contained in the plan.

The following Ten Egalitarian Commandments for

managers describe the essential principles that characterize many of the egalitarian companies in America, Obeying these commandments will help school administrators to reduce rank and status distinctions between themselves and their people and to treat their people fairly and impartially, in an effort to achieve excellence.

1. Thou shalt treat everyone as thou would like to be treated.
2. Thou shalt care, trust, and become intimate with school people.
3. Thou shalt recognize, praise, and reward school people.
4. Thou shalt encourage open communication.
5. Thou shalt share and equalize power with school people.
6. Thou shalt promote from within.
7. Thou shalt be tolerant of mistakes of school people.
8. Thou shalt expand the skills of school people through training, development, and education.
9. Thou shalt give school people autonomy to encourage intrapreneurship.
10. Thou shalt treat school people as members of thy family.

Strategies for Achieving Excellence

- Think of some egalitarian practices that you could institute in your school now and do so. Some examples: removing segregated parking spaces, referring to the superintendent by his or her first name, replacing partitions with open-space furniture, removing titles from doors, relaxing certain rules to diminish status or position differentials between school administrators and other school people.

- Permit teachers to prepare the lunch and duty schedule, after providing them with necessary parameters.

- In meeting with the central management team, use the nominal group process to arrive at a sublimity value statement. Develop a plan to promote the overriding value statement.

- Refer to all people on a building level as a "family."

- Establish a semi-annual newsletter that describes the results of efforts at egalitarianism, or the elimination of inegalitarian principles and practices.

Use a Personal Computer at the Top

More CEOs of Fortune 500 Companies are now using personal computers to communicate, gather crucial information and to develop strategies.
—Henry Fersko-Weiss

Recently I visited the office of a superintendent to look at his computer setup. Much to my surprise and dismay, he had no personal computer in his office. When I inquired as to why he did not have a personal computer, he said, "If I need information, I'll ask my business manager to get it for me." Although I have not conducted a study to determine whether this attitude is shared by the thousands of superintendents who lead our school districts, I suspect that it is by 95 to 99 percent of them. Most of those few who have a personal computer use it primarily as a means to keep tabs on the budget.

In many instances, the kids know more than their superintendent about the personal computer and have used it to better purpose. Since the main task of chief school administrators is making decisions, doesn't it seem logical that superintendents should take advantage of recent technological advancements to explore options, to analyze data, and to plan strategically and tactically? Shouldn't they use the new technology not only to keep track of finances but also for problem-solving, performance review, and other activities? Yes, it does seem logical, but superintendents have been slow to capitalize on the personal computer in their quest for excellence.

For people like Owen Butler, chairman of Procter & Gamble, Malcolm Stamper, president of Boeing, and John Curcio, chief executive officer of Mack Truck, Inc., and a growing number of like-minded chief executive officers of the best-run companies, the personal computer has become as vital a part of doing business, as essential as the telephone. Owen Butler, of Procter & Gamble maintains that the computer is a mind expander, and he should have access to it more than the top managers in a corporation, who presumably are more valuable in determining direction and improving profitability. Butler is an unusual manager because he had no previous experience in computers. However, he was so convinced that the chief executive officer should be competent in using the personal computer that he learned to use three computers and taught himself how to become a competent programmer. He did this by tinkering with his computer as a form of recreation. He produced skeletal programs and submitted them to his management department people, who elaborated and improved them. Recently, Butler developed a program to allow employees to use the computer to retrieve information pertaining to their retirement compensation plan. In addition, employees can use the program to enter estimates of future variables and see how these will affect their retirement benefits.

All chief executive officers play a pivotal role in the day-to-day communication process through the exchange of information with other top-level managers.

Finn Caspersen, chairman of Beneficial Corporation, maintains that he transmits and receives some 30 to 40 vital messages in a given day. To accommodate his communication needs, Caspersen uses the personal computer as a desk-top communication center. All inhouse memos, filing, room allocations, calendar entries, and meeting arrangements are done by his personal computer. He maintains "It's so much easier to schedule meetings because the machine does it for you. It will tell you at what hour all ten executives can get together, or when the six key executives are free. This job would normally take an hour and a half; now you have the answer in ten seconds." Caspersen is so enthralled with the system that he has installed an exact duplicate in his home. He says, "If I'm in a productive mood I can send instructions on a project or request some research at 5 o'clock in the morning or at night. Then my communication is there at the appropriate individual's work station when that person comes in."

In 1984, when Mack Truck and the UAW were in the midst of contract negotiation discussions regarding work rules, benefits, and other monetary items, John Curcio fed into his computer information received from the negotiation team housed in a Harrisburg hotel. Curcio spent 60 hours on call, feeding information into his computer, analyzing data, and giving feedback to the members of his team on the actual financial impact of the various proposals.

Before he had a personal computer, Boeing's president Malcolm Stamper used to write out all his speeches. He finds that with his personal computer he can organize his thoughts more easily and more quickly by adding ideas and changing sentences. Once he completes his speech, he files it away in the computer so that he can refer to it when he is working on a new speech. Another advantage of a personal computer is that it permits the chief executive officer to communicate from anywhere. Stamper takes his portable computer with him whenever he flies around the country. He maintains that he would rather leave home his American Express card than his computer. A portable personal computer gives the chief executive officer a direct link to virtually anybody within the company, no matter where in the world he or she is located.

One of the main reasons chief executive officers use the personal computer is to facilitate retrieval of information, particularly corporate financial data. With this information instantly accessible, they are able to diagnose the company's problems and identify solutions. Some chief executive officers also use their personal computers to maintain biographical information about people within and outside of the company. Robert Allen, chairman and chief executive officer of Carrier Corporation, has established a biographical database of nearly 1000 names, addresses, telephone numbers, and a code indicating each person's area of specialty. Allen maintains, "If I'm concerned with the housing situation in Phoenix, I can go into my database and see who I know in the construction business there. I can do this all over the world—when you travel you acquire a lot of calling cards."

Most of the chief executive officers who use the personal computer maintain that it has enabled them to improve their personal productivity substantially. Some report that it has given them greater flexibility in communicating with employees regardless of their location. Others indicate that it has given them sharper and more concrete approaches to solving company problems.

Some maintain that it has enhanced their ability to make better and faster decisions, and some state that it has given them an instrument to use in creating strategies and plans. Regardless of how the personal computer is used, it is a potent tool for chief executive officers of companies in search of excellence.

How Superintendents Can Make Use of the Personal Computer

How do I recommend that superintendents of schools make effective use of the personal computer? I think the best way for me to address this question is with a hypothetical case. Dr. John Byte was the superintendent of a medium-sized school district in Somewhere, USA. He first became interested in personal computers when he bought a small personal computer for his eleven-year-old daughter. Over the months his daughter became very proficient in using her computer and recently taught herself how to develop simple programs. One such program involved developing what she described as a "personal organizer." Through this program she scheduled her homework, television time, and leisure time.

Dr. Byte became so interested in the possibilities of computer programming that he decided to fortify himself with knowledge. He got the names and addresses of five computer experts and interviewed each of them with the help of one of the computer teachers in the district. After references were checked, the two of them reached a consensus on the top three consultants. Each of the consultants was asked to prepare a proposal for meeting the district's computer hardware, software, and training needs, as outlined by Dr. Byte. Because Dr. Byte wanted flexibility in customized software selection as well as in selection of program consultants, none of the customized software package requirements were included in his list of needs. The needs included a terminal for each building administrator as well as appropriate training. The proposals were critically reviewed, and Dr. Byte and the computer teacher selected the proposal that best met the needs and financial constraints of the school district.

The proposal was submitted to the board of education. Both Dr. Byte and the consultant responded to questions from the board. After the proposal was approved by the board, it was released to the general public for bidding purposes. After the best bid was approved by the board, Dr. Byte and school administrators received five days of training in use of the system.

One of the first programs Dr. Byte found vital to his day-to-day effectiveness was a desk management system. Through the use of this program he and his secretary were able to make appointments, perform some calculations, set meetings, input scratch information, receive telephone messages, and view a monthly calendar. A unique feature of this desk management program was that it allowed the superintendent to automatically dial selected telephone numbers. The daily schedule showed how appointments can be manipulated for automatic scheduling of meetings with all of district administrators. Calculations could be performed right on the monitor. A "things-to-do list," consisting of an electronic notepad with scrolling capability, allowed him to add to, delete, change, or print any or all items on the list. A telephone message pad allowed him to transfer messages to all school administrators within the school district. The calendar included a monthly display whereby Dr. Byte could scroll from one month to another. Dr. Byte used his desk management system to schedule the dates and times he would be devoting to management by wandering around. Using a pedometer he would then keep track of the mileage he allotted to this management practice. Each day he recorded the mileage on his calendar. At the end of each month his secretary made a tally of the daily figures and recorded it for comparison with the total for the succeeding month.

Since he was attempting to achieve excellence by implementing many of the lessons in this book, Dr. Byte wanted to use his computer to improve his contact with people throughout the district. The consultant suggested a word-processing program that displayed an entire page on the screen; checked and counted spelling errors; made simple grammatical corrections; contained a dictionary and a thesaurus; had mathematical and graphics capability as well as foreign-language capability; could build and maintain mailing, inventory, and membership lists; and could produce personalized letters, mailings, labels, and bibliographies.

Dr. Byte requested that his secretary go through all of the correspondence he sent to school people and select appropriate parts of letters to use in developing boilerplate paragraphs for future letters. From time to time he would add to this file. He also requested that a directory be made to store information from the more than 800 business cards he had collected over the years.

The superintendent had a extensive library in his office, and from time to time other school administrators would borrow his books and magazines without signing out for them. He requested that his secretary make a bibliography of all of his books and magazines and then devise some way for him to know who borrowed what and on what date. His secretary simply made a list of all of the superintendent's materials, and in the two columns adjacent to each book in the list, would indicate the name of the borrower and the date a book or magazine was borrowed. Later she revised this system so that the superintendent would get a monthly printout of the names of all school administrators and the titles of the books they had borrowed.

Throughout the year Dr. Byte received numerous brochures regarding conferences, seminars, workshops, and other training events he missed because they were over before he found out about them. To remedy this problem, he developed a computer file in which to store information on training and development events. The file included the date of each event, sponsoring organization, location, names, of the speakers, cost, and other relevant information. Each month, the computer generated a schedule of these events for Dr. Byte.

From time to time, the superintendent was called upon to deliver a major address to a large audience. Since he frequently used portions of one speech to complete another, he stored all of his presentations in the personal computer. To create a bibliography that would help him in preparing his presentations, he went through each book and magazine in his library and identified information on specific topics, such as consensus management, Theory Z, individualized learning, and staff absenteeism. The computer then correlated specific reading materials with each topic and created a file that included the quoted article, title, author, copyright date, and page number of each article.

The consultant identified two types of commercial software programs that Dr. Byte considered necessary to help him to manage the school district as it pursued excellence—a project planning program and a spreadsheet program. Dr. Byte had his research and development department study all of the available project planning software, submit a one-page analysis of each of five alternative software packages, rank the packages, and provide reasons for said rank. The package he selected offered all of the basic capabilities, such as planning by the critical path method, and much more. It enabled him to plan, organize, schedule, control, and monitor a project or program; focus on critical activities; input "what-if?" to analyze alternatives; communicate with principals; and improve presentations and proposals. The software placed as much emphasis on organizing ideas and thoughts as on scheduling and tracking projects. The package enabled him to generate a complete project plan after merely indicating activities and entering minimal predecessor information. With the use of this software package, Dr. Byte was able to generate flow charts and schedules automatically and to focus on any inconsistent information. Once the superintendent had been thoroughly trained and could use the package effectively, he required that all central administrators become fluent in the project-planning process and insisted that all projects and programs be planned using this package.

There are numerous spreadsheet software packages on the market, and Dr. Byte settled on the package that proved to be the most popular, based on sales. Dr. Byte found the spreadsheet an invaluable tool for determining enrollment projections, SAT score projections, and budget projections. The spreadsheet program was also a help in calculating whether to buy or lease certain types of equipment, determining socioeconomic trends over a five-year period, calculating the financial impact on the school district of a state voluntary early retirement law, projecting interest over a five-year period, determining the impact of escalating increases in hospitalization cost, and performing a host of other tasks.

To maximize the use of the personal computer, Dr. Byte realized that he could not merely rely on commercial software, so he made arrangements for the development of a number of customized software packages. The consultant had researched the commercial software on personnel absenteeism, but none of the available programs had the ability to produce a comprehensive history of a person's absentee record. So Dr. Byte retained one of the school district's computer specialists to prepare a district-wide absentee profile, and indicate monthly, year-to- date and historical absences. With the information arranged in this way, Dr. Byte could identify those school people responsible for 80 percent of the absences and direct principals to give them proper guidance and counseling, and he could send out appropriate letters to those school people with outstanding attendance records.

Another customized software package that Dr. Byte saw the need for was comprehensive strategic planning program, whose menu would include such items as the statement of the school district philosophy, competitive analyses, stakeholder analyses, contingency plans, financial data, scenarios, school district strengths and weaknesses, special problems, threats analyses, trend analyses, long-range goals, and program strategies. In addition, the program would also track year-to-year achievement of short-range objectives and indicate the extent to which long-range goals were being realized. Since changes were immediately inputted into the computer as they occurred, Dr. Byte was able to make more timely and better decisions using this program. In addition, problem areas were not allowed to slip by unnoticed.

Because the school district was committed to "growing its own" personnel, Dr. Byte found it necessary to get a customized succession software program, one that would track the growth and development of central administrators. The program was designed to store information on long-range human resource needs; career aspirations, interests, strengths, weaknesses, and talents; yearly performance outcomes; and education, training, and development activities. In addition, the program could generate a graphic illustration indicating how each central administrator was progressing along the long-range career path. The program kept track of training requirements for administrators and the degree to which these were being fulfilled. The succession program was maintained and updated by the human resources department. Using the program, the superintendent could determine at any time the progress of any central administrator and the degree to which the school district was "growing its own."

Once a superintendent begins to use the personal computer, he or she will likely become hooked on it. The more equipment is used, the more uses will be found for it. When used correctly and in a timely manner, a personal computer can minimize errors in judgment and help facilitate a school district's quest for excellence.

Strategies for Achieving Excellence

- Make use of the personal computer in project management to identify tasks, deadlines, and resources. With this information, you will be able to monitor the progress of important projects in the school district and take corrective action if performance is not as planned.

- Use the personal computer to analyze trends in various areas over a period of time. A computer will enable you to produce critical reports of the highest quality. You can show trends in funding by inserting a spread sheet, illustrate critical comparisons with a bar graph, highlight conclusions by creating a border of stars around them, and dramatize recommendations with artwork.

- Develop a high-quality school district newsletter using the personal computer.

- Encourage circle of excellence members to make use of the computer in identifying and selecting problems, collecting and analyzing data, and preparing charts, graphs, and scattergrams for use in solving problems.

- Learn to do simple programming.

- Arrange to attend one personal computer conference each year.

Become Research and Development Oriented

> The worst enemy of the best is the good enough; . . .
> Anything devised can be improved if people are
> given an opportunity to do so.
>
> —James J. Cribbin

The name of the game in public and private education for the 1980s and on into the twenty-first century is "innovate or decay." Rosabeth Moss Kanter, author of *The Change Masters*, maintains that "there is a clear and pressing need for more innovation, for we face social and economical changes of unprecedented magnitude and variety, which past practices cannot accommodate and which instead require innovative responses." Peter Drucker, the father of the science of management, states in his most recent book, *Innovation and Entrepreneurship*, "Unless it [the public school] takes the lead in innovation it is unlikely to survive the century, except as a school for minorities in the slums. For the first time in its history, the United States faces the threat of class structure in education in which all but the very poor remain outside of the public system— at least in the cities and suburbs where most of the population lives."

Schools Must Increase Innovation

To innovate, we must think and perform differently. Most innovations in public schools are imposed on the schools either by state departments of education, book publishers, regional service centers, and colleges and universities or by a catastrophe. If we are to survive in this rapidly changing society and meet the varied needs of our kids, we must give new emphasis to innovation and assume responsibility for our own fate instead of leaving it in the hands of others.

In *Achieving Excellence in Our Schools*, I strongly recommended organizing the teachers in each school building into teams and giving them the autonomy and freedom to become more creative and innovative. This is an attempt to get innovation moving on a building wide level. However, to get innovation moving on a district-wide level, we must establish a research and development component that is unlike the research and testing unit that some school districts have organized. The mission of most research and testing units is usually confined to studying the results of teaching efforts and determining what progress has been made. The research and development unit I am proposing would determine the needs of our kids and our school people and develop innovative programs, practices and products to meet those needs. Research and testing is an information service unit, whereas research and development is an action-oriented unit.

In the 1970s a large number of innovative programs, practices, and products were created in our public schools in part because billions of federal dollars were provided to public schools. When federal funds decreased so did innovations. Another factor contributing to the

74

demise of innovation in public education was that the innovations of the seventies were supported neither by strategy nor by a striving culture of the school districts. In many instances, innovations that were adopted represented a mismatch of the expectations of the board of education, the values of the superintendent, the culture of the school district, and the needs of students and teachers. Absolutely no innovation can be sustained for any length of time when such a tremendous mismatch exists.

There have been many studies on innovations. Among the most extensive studies of business innovation ever conducted were those performed by the noted economist Christopher Freeman. Freeman's studies indicated that the number one factor contributing to successful innovation in business was that successful companies understood the needs of their customers better than did the unsuccessful companies. The number two factor was the successful innovators innovated in response to customer needs and involved the potential customer in the development of the innovation. As we will see, these studies have implications for education.

The Research and Development Goals of the Best Companies

Let us consider the research and development goals of some of the best-run companies. Most of the research and development activities are defined under the term "innovation" and are included in statement of the company philosophy. For example, the statement of philosophy of Advanced Micro Devices read, "We share a commitment to innovation. We believe that to win in this industry, a company has to out-invest, out-produce, or out- innovate its competition." AMD chose to innovate. As an entre- preneurial entity with limited financial resources, ini- tially competing with established corporate giants who could both out-invest and out-produce us, we made the right choice . . . we put our fundamental focus on innovation with investment in research and devel- opment. . . ."

The statement goes on to say, "At AMD, we believe that growth springs from new ideas, from developing, nurturing and bringing to reality a new thought, or an improvement of an old one. We believe that growth follows innovation, Innovation has been AMD's formula for winning in our industry. . . . It is a strategy that has worked. Through innovation, we created a large portfolio of proprietary products that have increasingly contrib- uted to our sales. . . . AMD is growing every year because AMD people are innovative. And that means all AMD people, not just those involved in product development. We all contribute our thoughts, our ideas to ensure that AMD continues to grow and continues to be recognized as the best."

What do people at AMD say about innovation? A manager of electronic maintenance says, "At AMD, most of the improvement to our processes is the result of ideas from groups like our quality circles, or from individual production workers on the line. A lot of little sugges- tions—like moving a table 10 feet over to cut each worker's footsteps by 80 a shift. . . . "A job operator describes how improvements are made: "As an operator, I feel very much a part of the innovation that AMD is known for. When we started a new testing method for some of our wafers, an engineer asked me to help out. I inspected all of the wafers, then reported to him how I thought the process was working. My input as someone familiar with the day-to-day workings of the line was every bit as important to the overall project as the input of the team who developed it."

A supervisor of senior quality control was asked how the company was able to tackle a problem usually experienced by teachers when they get students from foreign countries in their classes: "When AMD opened its Penang plant in 1973, it was the first integrated circuit manufacturer in Malaysia; none of us who lived here even knew what an integrated circuit was. The workers had less education than American workers, and many of them didn't speak English. AMD took a unique approach to solving this problem with extensive training programs and quality programs that involved interpreters and multiple-language presentations. . . ." AMD makes a reality of its commitment to innovation through research and development by allocating an average of *16 percent* of its yearly sales research and development activities. In 1984, this amounted to over $100 million. According to a recent *Business Week* survey of the 800 top U.S. corporations in all industry categories, AMD ranks seventh in the nation in research and development spending as a percentage of sales.

Management at AMD measures "innovation productivity" to determine whether the company is increasing its innovative output. To do this, it compares how many productive innovations were introduced from one year to another. For example, in 1983, the company introduced 45 new products. In 1984, 56 new products were being planned.

IBM's goal in conducting research and development is to solve the increasingly complex problems of business, government, science, space exploration, defense, education, medicine, and many other areas of human activity. In 1983, IBM spent $3.6 billion on research and development, bringing the company's five-year investment in this area to $13.4 billion. What have been the results of IBM's research and development efforts? To mention a few:

- New telecommunications products and systems were produced that are tailored to meet the expanding needs of customers in the areas of manufacturing, finance, research, education, and government.

- Software was produced to increase the information-handling capacity of IBM's large-scale computers.

- The speed, capacity, and performance options available to users of mid-range and small-scale IBM computers were expanded.

- The IBM AT advanced-stage personal computer was introduced.

- The capabilities of IBM's office system offerings were extended, to improve the productivity of users and enable customers to plan and implement more efficient networks linking multiple locations within an organization.

- Database 2 and two related programs were introduced to offer large manufacturing, insurance, financial, and or public utility organizations easier access to data for strategic planning or day-to-day decision making.

- The company introduced the IBM 4730 personal banking machine, which can dispense exact change, cash paychecks, and accept check deposits without deposit slips or envelopes.

To remain competitive, Hewlett-Packard maintains a strong research and development program. In 1984 the company spent $592 million on research and development, nearly 10 percent of gross sales. Improving research and development productivity throughout the company is a priority. During 1983 the company began initiating in-depth seminars on research and development project management for nearly 4000 engineers and scientists involved in research and development activities. The courses helped to disseminate the best practices throughout the company. Hewlett-Packard also emphasized providing engineers with more and better tools for research and development, such as computer-aided design and engineering programs. The company established an Engineering Productivity Division to produce a stream of software products that will be used inside and outside of the company. A goal of Hewlett-Packard's research and development division is to design additional high-quality products that can be manufactured at lost cost. Researchers are achieving this goal by working closely with manufacturing throughout the development process and by designing products that are complex and yet easy to use. During 1983 Hewlett-Packard gave special emphasis within the computer groups to reducing the time required for designing new products. The result has been that more than 15 new major product programs were carried out within a period of one year.

I couldn't complete this section without saying a few words about 3M, one of the most innovative companies in the United States. Since its beginning, 3M has had a reputation for innovation. The company's first important product was a waterproof sandpaper that did away with the dust hazards associated with sanding automobiles. A few years later, the company made a breakthrough in automobile painting by producing the first pressure-sensitive masking tape. Since that time, the company's research and development efforts have produced hundreds of innovations, such as reflective sheetings for highway signs, magnetic tape for audio, video, and data recording, presensitized printing tape, and the popular Scotch brand transparent tapes. Innovation in research continues to result in problem-solving technologies and products at 3M. Some of the recent developments are as follows:

- The first tooth-colored dental filling durable enough to be used instead of gold or silver in posterior teeth.

- Very high-bond adhesives, which are so strong they are doing away with the need for mechanical fasteners in assembly jobs.

- An optical disk the size of a LP phonograph record that can store as much data as 20 rolls of computer tape.

What Can School Districts Do?

There are several things that people in the school districts can do to emulate the research and development efforts of the best-run companies.

First, acquire an understanding of research and development. Research and development is the process of determining a need of the school district and selecting or developing the most appropriate program, practice or product to accommodate that need. The research and development process will usually require innovation— that is, the introduction of something new, such as a new idea, method, or device. Innovation means more than modifying the way things are done in a school district. It requires some completely new elements, and it can be very risky. The success of an innovation is determined by seeing if it meets its intended purposes over a long period of time. Only with an in-depth understanding of what is involved in research and development will school administrators begin to acquire the commitment to it that is vital to taking one more step toward excellence.

Second, decide on a mission for the school district's research and development unit. Research and development activities should be focused on the attainment of the long-range goals of the organization. This division should by all means avoid being exclusively devoted to testing and measurement. The following example is a research and development unit:

It shall be the goal of this office to produce innovative programs, practices, and products that will assist teachers in the improvement of student learning and growth or will improve the management and operation of the school district. To this end, the staff will search out and locate problems within the school district through written and/or oral means and will identify alternative ways to solve problems by modifying, emulating, or creating programs, practices, or products within the constraints of the school district.

Third, see that the research and development unit has an adequate budget. The best-run companies make their research and development budgets a percentage of gross sales. I believe a good formula for setting an R&D budget for a school district is to allocate 25 dollars per student. Therefore, a district with three thousand students would have a research and development budget of $75,000. A large school district could reduce this student allocation to $5 or $10 per student. Based on these guidelines the annual R&D budget for a school district of 500,000 students would be between $2.5 and $5 million.

Fourth, adequately staff the research and development unit. Rather than identifying the various positions to be included on the staff, I think it is more important to identify the types of people and kinds of experience needed to make the R&D unit functional.

- A school executive champion.

- School program champions.

- A person who has been certified as a quality circle facilitator or someone with similar qualifications and experience in problem solving.

- A person who has had editorial and promotional experience in publishing.

- A person who has had experience creating and developing educational products.

- A person who has had experience in developing, administering, and analyzing surveys, questionnaires, and other instruments to determine needs.

Fifth, become knowledgeable about indicators of changes that have already occurred within or outside of your district and of those that could be brought about with little effort, as such changes often provide opportunities for innovation.

Internal Sources
- Unexpected events. When an unexpected event occurs, capitalize on the success, learn from the failure, or make the most of the opportunities created by the outside event through innovation.

- Incongruity. When there is a significant variant between the theory and what actually exists, a need exists to close the gap through innovation.

- Process needs. When a problem exists in the way something is done, a need exists to create a process to solve the problem through innovation.

- Organizational structural changes. When structural changes have occurred, there is a need for innovative changes in people's performance.

External sources
- Population shifts. When changes in demographics threaten performance results, a need exists to make the most of the opportunity through innovation.

- Changes in perception and mood. When changes in people's perceptions and moods threaten the operation of the organization, there is a need to review the behavioral and attitudinal changes and to develop ways to deal with them in a positive manner through innovation.

- New knowledge. When new knowledge develops, a need exists to capitalize on the new knowledge through innovation.

Sixth, understand Peter Drucker's theory of innovations. Drucker postulates the following conditions for making innovations work:

- Innovation requires hard work. Innovation requires knowledge and quite often a great deal of ingenuity. Some people tend to be more talented innovators than others. The talented innovators are the ones we should search out. When innovating it is best for the innovator to concentrate on one innovation at a time. The persons who are selected to be in an R&D unit not only must be talented, but also must be diligent pursuers of a goal, persistent under difficulties, and committed to the mission of the unit.

- Innovation must build on strengths. Innovators carefully make use of the multitude of opportunities made available to them. They look for the proper fit between what the kids need, what the district is good at, and what resources are available to create an innovative solution to a problem.

Peter Drucker also identifies some do's and don'ts regarding the principles of innovation that I think deserve some attention.

The Do's
- Do think through the sources of innovative opportunities.

- School administrators should organize a search of innovative opportunities and perform it on a regular and systematic basis.

- Do consult others. Going to kids, teachers, and other school people in the course of conducting the search. Both the left side and the right side of the brain should be used—that is, equal concern should be given to both people and hard facts.

- Do start small by attempting to do only one thing. When I train school administrators in the quality concept, I recommend that they start with no more than four to six quality circles. In that case, if a change has to be made, it does not have to be done on a large scale.

- Do aim the innovation at leadership.

The Don'ts
- Don't try to be too smart or clever. Innovations are implemented by normal human beings. If situations become complicated, the innovations will be most likely to fail.

- Don't try to do too many things at one time.

- Don't innovate only for the present without thinking about the future.

An innovation is a change. It may be a change in the behavior of kids, school people, community members, or people in general. It may also be a change in process— that is, how people work and create something. To be effective, innovation in schools must be close to kids, focused on kids, and indeed kid-driven.

Strategies for Achieving Excellence

- Interview kids and use other means to determine their needs in order to generate ideas for innovations.

- Interview parents who are sending their children to private school in order to get ideas for innovations.

- Involve kids in the development of innovation.

- Conduct an audit of schools and departments to list the number of innovative programs, practices and products produced throughout the previous school year. Use this list to discuss with your administrators the extent to which the school district engages in innovation to improve student learning and growth. Discuss what efforts should be made to be more responsive to the needs of kids through innovation.

- Visit the innovative companies in this lesson, particularly 3M, and see what you can learn from their innovative efforts.

- Conduct a minimum of three one-day meetings during the school year in which teams are organized by topics or subject areas to meet to generate innovative ideas on a district-wide level. Prior to the meeting, designate and train team leaders in brainstorming and the nominal group process. Use these processes for generating innovative ideas.

- Organize an innovation committee consisting of a majority of teachers, if innovation in teaching is the goal, or a majority of administrators, if innovation in administration is the goal. Have this committee develop requirements for submitting proposals for new programs, practices, and products, and list the factors that will be considered in judging the value of a proposed innovation. Committee members should be required to rate each proposal separately and bring their findings to the committee meeting for discussion. The best proposals should be recommended to the research and development unit for a feasibility study. The research and development department should be required to submit its recommendations to the innovation committee, which will then make the final decision.

- Visit a competing school district. Prepare a statement of its operations that describes its practices, products, programs, and management style. Identify those strategic areas where the school district excels, then select and implement an innovation that will enable you to outperform your competition.

• Lesson 6 •

Revamp the Process of Selecting Teachers

Teaching is not a career for the unconcerned or the uncommitted. Only the most talented . . . young men and women should be granted the opportunity to become classroom teachers.

—Mary H. Futrell

The term "revamp" means to renovate or revise and this is exactly what I think should be done with the methods presently used by school districts throughout the country to select teachers. As a nation-wide consultant, I get lots of opportunities to visit schools and witness teachers in action. At times I am amazed at the vast number of incompetent teachers our kids are being exposed to—teachers who cannot speak well, teachers who cannot write a simple sentence without an error, teachers who just don't know how to teach. I call these teachers "play teachers"; they play at the profession of teaching.

The problem of incompetent teachers is a national one and will require creative and innovative solutions. Recently Albert Shanker, president of the American Federation of Teachers, proposed that aspiring teachers be required to pass a tough national test. Shanker proposed a three-part licensing exam. The first part would consist of a rigorous written test of the candidate's knowledge of their subject area. The second part would consist of a written and an oral test to determine a candidate's knowledge of the principles of education; it would cover subjects such as effective teaching and classroom management. The third part of the test would involve the candidate in a supervised internship covering a period of one to three years. I believe that Shanker should be applauded for his proposal and that union officials everywhere should become as concerned about upgrading the image of teachers as they are about protecting teachers from insensitive school administrators.

I think Shanker's proposal is a step in the right direction. It is not sufficient, however, to ensure competence. There is no substitute for a rigorous teacher-selection program in each school district.

Eight Steps to Selecting Better Teachers

My study of the best-run companies indicates that there are eight steps that school districts should take in selecting new teachers.

The first step is a base and sets the tone for the entire teacher-selection process by including in the statement of the school district an explicit description of the philosophy desired by the district. The goal here is to inculcate throughout the culture of the school district those attributes and traits that the school district is looking for when selecting teachers and other school people.

The New Jersey State Department of Education has established an alternative teacher-certification program in an effort to address the current teacher shortage as well as to improve teacher education. One component of this program calls for prospective teachers to spend more time in a classroom setting. On the whole, nothing seems wrong with this idea. However, a very large percentage of the prospective teachers in one of the state's urban school districts left their schools, never to return to education. The problem was that the cultural orientation of the prospective teachers was incompatible with that of the school district, which has a substantial minority population. I maintain that if a cultural orientation test were administered to prospective teachers before they became intimately involved with a student body, those persons whose cultural orientations were not consonant with that of the school district could be weeded out. These people need not leave education—they may be able to become outstanding teachers in a school district with a cultural orientation more in line with their own.

The founders of Procter & Gamble laid the foundation that enabled it to become one of America's best-run companies by including in the statement of the company's philosophy a description of the kind of employees the company would seek: "Find and hire people—people with character who want only the opportunity to develop themselves to the best of their abilities." Celestial Seasonings' company philosophy is even more explicit: "We believe in hiring above-average people who are willing to work for excellent results. In exchange, we are committed to the development of our good people by identifying, cultivating, training, retraining, and encouraging those individuals who are committed to moving our organization forward."

The second step in a teacher-selection process should be to recruit unspoiled teacher candidates. By "unspoiled" I mean candidates who are recent graduates of teacher-training institutions. A school district should be committed to "growing its own"; it should seek candidates who have not developed bad practices that would necessitate a "decontamination process." It is easier to inculcate a desired culture when you don't have to undo old and unacceptable work habits.

Like other best-run companies, Nissan recruits college graduates with general backgrounds and teaches them a broad range of business and job-related skills. During one year, Procter & Gamble conducted 29,000 interviews at 250 college university campuses to fill fewer than 1000 entry-level positions. Obviously P&G takes recruitment very seriously. A good recruitment strategy for a school district would be to distribute to students enrolled in teacher-training programs highly professional printed materials illustrating various programs and practices of the school district. Another strategy would be to have selected teachers from the district level to travel with the district's human resource staff to discuss the particulars of the school district with potential candidates.

The third step in the selection process should be to test the candidates. Good speaking and writing skills are essential for all teachers; therefore, the first test should require the candidate to demonstrate acceptable speaking and writing skills. If a candidate does not show minimal competency in both of these areas, he or she should not be permitted to continue in the selection process. A candidate need not be an excellent speaker or writer, but should be at such a level that the school district can provide help without expending a large amount of time, money, and effort. The writing portion of the test should not be similar to the one given with the national teachers examination, but should be more of a competency and diagnostic test to point out areas needing improvement. Sometimes a candidate who is strong in other aspects of the selection process may barely reach minimal competency levels in speaking and writing. If a decision is made to hire a particular candidate despite weaknesses in these skills, the school district will need to assume responsibility for strengthening the new teacher's skills through a pre-teaching program, in which the new teacher receives extensive training in speaking and writing before entering the classroom. The length of the pre-teaching program should be dependent on the individual needs of each new teacher.

The second test should be a personality test designed to determine if the candidate can get along with colleagues and kids. The district should either develop or obtain a personality test that measures whether or not a candidate's personality is compatible with the existing culture of the school district. This factor has rarely gotten much attention in school districts, and it is high time that it did.

A growing number of companies around the nation have found personality tests effective not only for selecting employees, but also for getting the most out of them. H. Parker-Sharpe, Inc. administers a personality test known as the Beakman Method for potential employees. In one case the company gave this test to a man applying for position as an insurance agent. At his former job, the applicant had sold only $260,000 worth of insurance in six months. However, the personality test revealed that if the applicant were closely supervised and recognized and praised for his achievement, he would thrive. The company hired the applicant, gave him a plush office, closely monitored his activities, and treated him well. Within six months, the salesman had sold $2.2 million worth of insurance.

The third test given to each candidate should be an interest test. The school district is looking to capitalize on the strengths, talents, and skills of each teacher. It is assumed that by pinpointing each candidate's interests, the district will be able to identify areas where he or she excels and will be able to capitalize on them.

The fourth step in the selection process should be to contact the applicant's references by telephone. It is not a good idea to rely on written references; far too many school administrators are willing to write glowing letters to get rid of incompetent teachers. I have found through experience that if you ask the right questions of the person named as a reference, you will be able to detect how the person actually feels about a particular teacher. For example, you might ask, "Would you trust this candidate with your life? Why?" "How would you use this candidate as a role model for other teachers"? "On a scale of one to ten, how would you rate this candidate?" (If responses are acceptable, I usually consider a rating of nine or ten to be acceptable), I continue probing to satisfy any particular concerns I have.

The fifth step in the selection process should be to interview candidates. This step should be accomplished by the central administrators as well as the building principal and the teaching team. On the central-administration level, each candidate should get a cursory interview as a means of determining in what particular school and with what school administrator he or she would work well. On the school and team levels the interviews should be more comprehensive and more grueling. The principal should conduct initial interviews on this level and present his or her list of candidates to the team having the vacancy. Team members should meet as a team prior to the interview to discuss the credentials, test results, strengths, and talents of each candidate. At the interview, team members should use the statement of the district's philosophy to determine whether the candidate's personality is compatible with the school district's culture, should make their own observations of the candidate's speaking and writing proficiency and specific interests, should consider whether the candidate will add to or subtract to the harmony and synergy of the team, and should focus on how the candidate's strengths can complement any weaknesses of the team. The team should realize that the responsibility for hiring a team member is an important one, and should be willing to devote as much time as necessary.

The people of Apple Computer use the company's values statement during interviews to determine if candidates are compatible with the company's culture. Sometimes the interview process is long and arduous, involving multiple sessions. Ann Bower, who operates Apple University, maintains that the company is " . . . looking for people who are coaches and team builders and expanders, not controllers of people."

It is extremely difficult to get hired at Bell Laboratories. If a candidate is fortunate enough to get to the interview stage, he or she is interviewed by five or six people from the lab most likely to hire the candidate. The culture of each lab varies with the people. Therefore, in order to determine if the candidate's personality can accommodate the culture, an intense interviewing process is needed.

Raychem Corporation's employees take the interviewing process seriously. It is not unusual for a candidate in an engineering job to meet individually for an hour or more with each of 10 to 12 managers before a decision is made about hiring him or her.

Over the years I have interviewed hundreds of candidates for all types of positions. I usually look for those who are people oriented and result oriented. I try to get their reactions to a question such as "What is your major strength?" I have found that "I get along well with people" is almost a standard reply. I then ask the candidate, "What is your major weakness?" If the response does not cite strength as a weakness, as in "I tend to be impatient with mediocrity," I will ask another question, such as "If you had only one hour to live, what would you do?" In asking this question, I am looking for an answer indicating that the candidate is dedicated to serving people other than her or his family. Process-oriented people will usually say something like "I'd spend it with my family," or "I'd spend it at the beach reading a good book." Results-oriented people will usually say something like "I would think about a major goal or objective that I had not achieved and would attempt to take care of it," or "I would write a book that would be of invaluable interest to a large segment of population." The interviewing session can be a powerful tool in screening out undesirable candidates, provided appropriate questions are asked. The problem is that most interviewers, including board members, school administrators, and teachers, don't take the time necessary to devise thought-provoking questions that bring out the "person" in the interviewee.

The sixth step in the teacher-selection process should be to reach a consensus on candidates. I believe that efforts to achieve excellence are enhanced when decisions are reached by consensus. Since team members will be those directly affected by the caliber of persons hired, they should make the final decision who is hired for team membership. A growing number of the best-run companies, such as Apple Computer, Kollmorgen, Electro-Scientific Industries, and Exxon, are using consensus for selecting candidates for jobs.

The seventh step should be to provide an adequate orientation program for all newly hired teachers. Most school-district orientation programs last from a few hours to a day. If the best-run companies are any indication, school districts are seriously lacking in this area. In many companies, newly hired people get intensive instruction that last from several days to a month or more. An important feature of the orientation program is a presentation conducted by the chief executive officer concerning the philosophy, the culture, and the strategy of the organization. Not only should each newly hired teacher get a chance to meet the highest-ranking official of the school, but each person should receive an "uncoated" version of the way things are done in the school district and a description of the expectations of all school people. I think it makes good sense to include the orientation program as a part of the pre-teaching program so as to give the pre-teaching program a proper focus.

Once a decision has been made to hire a candidate, the eight steps are to upgrade the person's entry-level skills through training. The three-step testing may have revealed that certain of the candidate's skills should be upgraded. The pre-teaching program should be used for this purpose; it should be seen as a way to cultivate in the new teacher an understanding of the ways things are to be done in the school district. The program should be rigorous and should require each candidate to receive training in all areas needing improvement and to back up the training with actual practice in the classroom. The director of the pre-teaching program should be held responsible for making sure each new teacher develops acceptable teaching behavior. Once each candidate has acquired all of the entry-level teaching skills, he or she should be assigned to a team.

You might be wondering, "What do we do with the results of the national teacher examination proposed by Albert Shanker?" The results of this test, as well as undergraduate and graduate records and grades, student-teaching evaluations, and other information about a job candidate, should be used as criteria for determining whether a candidate meets minimal background requirements. This information will provide the starting point for the teacher-selection process.

The selection process that I have described is based on four assumptions: first, that the school district is fully aware of the large number of incompetent teachers who are entering the portals of our school buildings and is committed to doing something innovative about remedying the situation; second, that the school district is committed to "growing its own": third, that the school district is ready, willing, and able to support its commitment with the guts and funds that will be required; fourth, that the school district is willing to integrate its long-range personnel needs with a strategic career-path program, a comprehensive training program, and a well-planned succession program, all in an effort to achieve excellence.

Strategies for Achieving Excellence

- Visit two to three professional agencies and interview the people in charge in order to learn how the professionals go about selecting people for various positions. Make certain that someone in the agency specializes in selecting chief executive officers for corporations.

- Obtain a copy of each of the following personality tests, critically review them and either select the one that best meets your needs or develop your own personality test using the list as a base for information.

  — California Psychological Inventory
  — Gordon Personal Profile
  — Guilford-Zimmerman Temperament Survey
  — Minnesota Multiphasic Personality Inventory
  — Thorston Temperament Schedule

- If you develop your own personality test, use the school district's statement of philosophy to guide you. Then have an expert on the preparation of psychological instruments determine whether the instrument is valid and reliable. Interview to determine whether the candidate's personality is compatible with values and norms of the school district. Retain an expert in the preparation of psychological instruments to determine if the instrument is valid and reliable.

- Include a psychologist at every interviewing session. He or she should be called upon to give his or her impression of the personality of the candidate.

Establish a Holistic Relationship with the Community

Trust and understanding grow where individuals are linked to one another through multiple bonds in a holistic relationship.

— William Ouchi

Most school districts display an attitude that William Ouchi, author of Theory Z calls "partial inclusion." They believe that the connection between school districts and communities should be limited to those activities that are directly related to the education of kids. I maintain that it is the duty of the school district to become involved in the pressing needs of the community. In 1967, when I became the chief executive administrator of a small school district, one of the first things I did was take a tour of the homes of some of my students. I was so appalled at what I saw that I requested that the commissioner of social services and the commissioner of health accompany me on a subsequent tour. In addition, I requested that the school district's social worker invite the press to visit the homes with us. I pointed out how atrocious living conditions were for my students. Many of the homes had broken windows, leaking roofs, no heat, and broken-down walls. In some instances, an entire family used one bed. In other instances, eating utensils were at a minimum, and the children had to wait until other members of the family had finished eating before they could eat. Some parents were ashamed to open up their homes to us. However, because our social worker did her job well, we were admitted, with much reservation. The press had a field day. I prompted parents to relate their trials and tribulations to the commissioners. Some parents wept as they told of the difficulties they were experiencing in providing adequate living conditions for their children. My intent in conducting the home tours and inviting the press was to sensitize the people who had some control over the conditions besetting the families of my students. What was the effect of the tour? There were several. Community people knew they had a powerful conduit (my office) to the commissioner of the health and social service agencies which could be used in the event of an emergency or a serious event. Community health agencies were more responsive and aggressive in meeting the health needs of kids in the school district. Emergency checks for the families were able to be processed at a more rapid rate than previously. More parents participated in school affairs. Pressure was put on landlords to improve the housing conditions for tenants or face a fine and/or jail.

The day after the tour, the press devoted nearly an entire page to the horrendous living conditions of families in the district. I felt good about what I had done; this was my first move in becoming involved in the affairs of the community.

The tour took place before Thanksgiving. I knew that for many of my students this holiday would have very little meaning; there would be no thanks in their

Thanksgiving. I spoke to the district's business manager and explained that I wanted to use my office to solicit money from the district's suppliers so that some of my students could enjoy a Thanksgiving dinner. He thought little of the idea, but agreed to cooperate. I also contacted my social worker, who thought the idea was excellent. Rather than dispatch a letter to our dealers, my business manager and I personally contacted about forty of them. My social worker contacted the community action committee and told the members what we were doing; they happily agreed to help us with this project. We collected nearly a thousand dollars. The money was given to the community action committee, which bought the turkeys and other food and packed the food in bags. I called a special meeting of my administrators and suggested that we use our individual vehicles to collect the bags of food from the community action committee and deliver them to the homes of those most in need. My administrators and I took off in our cars and delivered bags of food to more than one hundred homes. Several days after the delivery, I was severely reprimanded by the president of the board, who felt that community affairs were not the province of the school district, but that didn't really bother me. When I sat down to have Thanksgiving with my family, I felt good, because I knew that many of my other families were enjoying a turkey on Thanksgiving, some for the first time in their lives.

How the Best Become Involved in the Community

We can learn much about what is meant by a holistic relationship with the community by examining how the best-run companies become actively involved in their communities.

Hewlett-Packard identifies its commitment to the community in its statement of corporate objectives, which is one of the most comprehensive of those of the best-run companies. According to the statement, it is the company's objective "to honor our obligations to society by being an economic, intellectual and social asset to each community in which we operate." The objective is then further clarified: "We must make sure that each of these communities is better for our presence. This means identifying our interests . . . with those of the community; it means contributing talent, time, and financial support to worthwhile community projects."

The statement continues: "Each community has its particular set of social problems. Our company must help to solve these problems. As a major step in this direction, we must strive to provide worthwhile employment opportunities for people of widely different backgrounds. Among other things, this requires positive action to seek out and employ members of disadvantaged groups, and to encourage and guide their progress toward full participation at all position levels."

"As citizens of their community, there is much that people can and should do to improve it—either working as individuals or through such groups as churches, schools, civic or charitable organizations. In a broader sense, HP's 'community' also includes a number of business and professional organizations, such as engineering and scientific societies, whose interests are closely identified with those of the company and its individual employees. These, too, are deserving of our support and participation. In all cases, supervisors should encourage HP people to fulfill their personal goals and aspirations in the community as well as attain their individual objectives within HP."

Atlantic Richfield encourages its people to work for community groups by giving annual community service awards to employees who have made outstanding contributions to the community. Periodically, the company publishes a report called "Participation" which contains information on its community activities.

H. B. Fuller Company is another one of the best-run companies that believes in community participation. Each year it encourages its people to participate in community activities by presenting an Outstanding Volunteer Award to the employee who has done the most for the community. At Christmas, through the company's "Filler-Up Program," employees collect toys and food for distribution to the poor. (This activity is similar to one conducted by students of the John F. Kennedy High School of New York City, under the direction of principal Robert Mastruzzi. At Christmas the students collect hundreds of gifts to be distributed to needy children. This event has become a traditional holiday ritual, and the students take great pains in wrapping each gift and delivering it themselves). Also, each plant elects a local community affairs committee to disburse money from the company's charity fund. For the past few years, the chairperson of the local community affairs committees have decided to fund activities involving battered women and child abuse. The company's Rape and Sexual Assault Legal Advocate Program has received nationwide fame.

Chairman James L. Ketelson of Tenneco Inc. spends about a third of his time getting company people involved in community affairs. More than 1500 people participate in a variety of volunteer programs through which they help disabled children, work with the retarded, and assist senior citizens. In addition, employees are involved in fund-raising telethons on the local educational TV channel. In 1982 Tenneco became the only private company to receive a presidential citation for its participation in community affairs.

Two companies that should be mentioned in any discussion of participation in community affairs are IBM and Hallmark. In 1983 IBM participated in a number of community programs. It provided support to a nationwide drug awareness program through which teachers' guides and classroom materials dealing with devastating effects of drug abuse were distributed to 35,000 schools. IBM also provided support to nonprofit organizations working on an assortment of problems including delivering health care and social services to senior citizens and handicapped people and improving housing in inner-city neighborhoods.

Dan Hall, chairman of the board of Hallmark, expresses the philosophy of this best-run company in this way: "When Hallmark speaks of social responsibility, we don't mean truth in advertising, job safety, or equal opportunity. These are legal and moral obligations that are accepted and expected. . . . Rather, I like to think in terms of a higher standard which defines social responsibility or social opportunity: the opportunity to bring the resources and skill of business people to bear on community problems. It is a standard which encourages Hallmarkers to be involved in community activities. . . . The company should use its talents and resources to benefit its communities."

Hallmark makes a reality of this standard by becoming involved in a number of community activities. In 1969, when a tornado devastated the Hickman Mills section of Kansas City, Hallmarkers were dispatched to help out with a single directive: "Find people and give them whatever help they need." Throughout the stormy night and the following days, hundreds of Hallmark people worked in the community, cleaning up wreckage and giving comfort and emergency relief to those whose homes had been damaged or lost. (The response at Hallmark is in marked contrast to that of a middle school principal in the northeast when a storm ripped down trees and telephone poles and flooded not only the streets, but also the homes of hundreds of community members. When several teachers called the principal and told him of the difficulties they were encountering as a result of the storm, his response was in effect, that he was able to arrive at school on time and so could they.)

In cities where Hallmark's facilities are located, contributing committees distribute community grants based on the needs of the people in the communities. The committees may provide matching grants to aid education programs, support for clinics or day-care facilities for children or senior citizens, funds for drug rehabilitation or child abuse prevention and treatment projects. Providing money to support worthy community projects is only part of Hallmark's commitment to the community. Personal involvement in the community by the people of Hallmark is also important. People at all levels of the company volunteer their time to participate in all sorts of community activities, from serving on boards of directors to visiting with prison inmates. Some Hallmarkers help to balance the budget of city-wide agencies, while others create handmade gifts for hospitalized children.

Another belief at Hallmark is that the finest thing the company can do for the community is to "create a quality employment goal for all people so they can build economic security for themselves and their children."

An interdependent relationship also exists between Procter & Gamble and the communities where the company's facilities are located. The company's support for education, the arts, and civic, health, and social service activities help enhance the community. To help build support for Procter & Gamble, the company encourages its people and managers to participate in community activities. In 1977, Procter & Gamble helped to establish the Cincinnati Business Committee. This committee tries to find ways to solve complex community problems related to education, government effectiveness, transportation, and revitalization of the downtown area.

General Mills is another company that takes community involvement seriously. In 1981, it established an "external involvement program" whereby at the beginning of each year each manager must state his or her plans to get involved in the community. Participation can mean volunteering to work with the local Red Cross Chapter or the United Way, or locating people to volunteer their time to work on specific community projects.

Good Things Happen Within a Holistic Environment

When a school district maintains a holistic relationship with the community, people within and outside the school district are more likely to participate in all school as well as community affairs. The vast resources of the total community are made available to all social agencies, to improve the health and welfare of all people of the community. This holistic relationship creates conditions in which depersonalization is at a minimum, caring is at a maximum, autocracy is unlikely, trust is more likely and an attitude of "we are all in this together" is common. The whole school district consists not only of the schools, but also of the parents, the citizens, and the community.

A holistic relationship is a consequence rather than a cause of school district and community interaction. The school administrator cannot simply say, "We promote a holistic relationship with our community" and expect it to be true. It is the school-community interaction that will *create* the holistic environment. This interaction will help to establish an egalitarian environment by bringing school people and community people together as equals, regardless of socio-economic status, and thus demonstrate that the distance between them is neither great nor impossible to embrace. School integration through holism will enable school administrators to see community groups and community champions as vital resources for the improvement of the educational process as the school district advances toward excellence.

A holistic relationship between the school district and the community will benefit both parties. School people and community people will begin to know more about each other, talk about a greater variety of subjects, and become involved in a wider range of educational and community activities. Members of the community will display less anxiety, isolation, and hostility toward the school district. School administrators will fear community champions less. School people and community people will develop a healthier working relationship and a more positive frame of mind.

What School Districts Can Do

What strategies can our school district borrow from the best-run companies in an effort to establish a holistic relationship with the community? There are several—let me suggest a few:

- Identify in the statement of philosophy the school district's commitment to the community, and some of the types of community activities the school district will participate in.

- Open the school district up to the community, as has been done in Atlantic City, New Jersey. For example, the community might be invited to participate in a comprehensive "Wellness Program" involving dental and medical care, counseling, physical fitness and dieting classes, etc. comprehensive, involving dental, medical, counseling, physical fitness, dieting, etc.

- Meet on a regular basis with various community groups to determine their needs, indicate your needs, and identify how you can help each other.

- Publicize the district's goal of establishing a holistic relationship with the community, and make sure that that it becomes an important and accepted value within the school district.

- Use school administrators as school "disciples" to unite the school district with the community. Insist that they develop plans at the beginning of the school year to work on community projects.

- Provide for awards to be given to the school people who have done the most for the community and the community people who have done the most for the school district.

- Arrange for school officials and community leaders to meet twice a year with the leaders of social agencies to address the macroscopic and microscopic needs of the community and the school district.

Strategies for Achieving Excellence

- Prepare a stakeholders' analysis that identifies major community stakeholders and their attitudes and expectations and specifies any actions to be taken by the school district based on these attitudes and expectations. Meet with major stakeholders to present this analysis, and discuss how each group can help the other, and develop and execute plans for aiding both the school and community.

- Conduct a critical analysis of community needs, citing major strengths and weaknesses of the community and indicating actions to be taken. Discuss this analysis with school administrators and ask for volunteers to assume responsibility for taking appropriate action to accommodate each major activity.

- Require that each school develop a plan for becoming involved in the community by assuming responsibility for a major community project. Get community people committed to the project. Evaluate and report the results of the project in the local newspaper.

- Establish a "Social Benefits Program" similar to the one organized by the Levi Strauss Company, whereby company people are encouraged to be active in community activities. (Under this program, a Levi Strauss employee who is active in a community group or agency for at least a year may request the Levi Strauss foundation to make a contribution of $500 to an agency with a budget up to $100,000; $1,000 to an agency with a budget between $100,000 and $1 million, and $1,500 to an agency with a budget over $1 million.) Ask local dealers to contribute to the fund, or suggest that school groups engage in fund raising activities to support the program, perhaps in cooperation with community groups.

• Lesson 8 •

Disseminate an Informative Annual Report

An up-to-date annual report can be a strong, interesting, and convincing review of the company, weld-
ing together, for the good of the corporation, all the
elements on which it depends.

—Leland Brown

You might think that something as simple as an
annual report would not pose a serious problem for
school administrators, but this is not the case. Some
superintendents have not found it fitting to inform their
stakeholders about the annual progress of the school
district. Other top school administrators are not aware
of what information should go into an annual report.
Those reports that are disseminated are often poorly
organized, written, designed, and duplicated. And,
finally, those superintendents who have produced excellent annual reports (and some have actually won
public relations awards) don't disseminate them to all of
the people who should receive them. Usually, school
people either don't receive annual reports or are the last
to get them.

Annual Reports of the Best

Procter & Gamble's 1984 Annual Report contains three major sections. The first section covers information pertaining to operations. A subsection includes financial highlights and information on United States business, international operations, long-term growth, financial strengths, capital expenditures, research and development, federal deficits, and organizational changes. The second section contains information on five important new brands that were sold nationally. The third section contains financial statements, including a statement of earnings, a report by independent accountants, a financial review of the years 1969-1984, supplemental information on the effects of inflation and changing costs, and shareholders' information. Sections one and three of the report are printed in one color, and section two is highlighted in multiple colors.

An interesting feature of Procter & Gamble's annual report is that a portion of the first section is devoted to organizational changes such as retirements, promotions, and changes in the board of directors.

Hewlett-Packard has an attractive annual report. Its 1984 report is similar to those of other best-run companies, and contains two major sections: (1) company operations and (2) financial statements. The front page is devoted to a description of what the company does and to financial highlights. Next follows a message to shareholders in which new product development is featured, marketing emphasis is discussed, changes in the board of directors are explained, and the company's outlook for the future is described. The first section of the report also includes a discussion of the company's commitment to its customers and its operations. The financial statements section contains the standard financial information. The final portion of this section contains shareholder information, year-in-review, and names of the directors and officers. Most of Hewlett-Packard's report is printed in maroon and black ink on buff paper, and the first section contains a number of multi-colored pictures of designs, products, and people.

The first page of IBM's 1984 annual report contains financial highlights for the year, contrasting the previous year's gain with the current year's. The next few pages contain a message to the stockholders about long-term prospects, continued growth, product leadership, increased efficiency, profitability, the importance of quality, merger information, and the election of a new chief executive officer. Immediately after this section is a description of what was done to assure effective administration of internal controls and then a statement by independent accountants.

Hallmark produces an interesting annual report. It does not include any financial information, primarily because Hallmark is not a public company. Instead, each annual report has a theme. In 1983, the theme was "A Commitment to Excellence." With the exception of the first section, which contains the names of the board of directors and some facts about Hallmark, each section of the 1983 annual report deals in some way with excellence, describing the company's commitment to continued excellence and ways in which excellence was attained in retail environments, in design and execution, in retailing to mass merchandisers, in international and subsidiary operations, in advertising, in industrial and office design, and in community involvement. The cover of Hallmark's 1983 annual report is rather simple, but elegant, consisting of a crown (the company's logo) embossed in gold within a two-and-a-half-inch blue square. The lettering is in gold. Inside the annual report are numerous multi-color pictures of Hallmark's people, products, operations, and various activities.

One of the best designed annual reports that I have come across is the 1984 Annual Report of Apple Computer. On the front cover is a photo of the Macintosh computer. The inside of the cover contains three quotes from IBM management to the effect that the company expects its large processors and mainframes to be responsible for its continued growth, and not the personal computer. Opposite the IBM quotes are two quotes to the effect that the personal computer "is the heart of Apple." The next several pages contain 1984 financial highlights, some photographs of memorable television images that marketed Apple products, a message to shareholders that describes a new product strategy, photos of the chairman of the board and the chief executive officer, and images of Apple products as well as of four students using the Apple II. Several pages are then devoted to the various teams that make up the company. The left pages of this section contain information regarding each team, and the right pages include pictures and names of team members. The next section of the report contains the kinds of financial statements usually found in annual reports. Usually an annual report ends with the financial section. Not so with Apple Computer's. This annual report ends with a section that displays on the left pages pictures of various professional people who have used the Macintosh, and on the right pages photos indicating how the Macintosh was used. For example, Ted Turner, the entrepreneur and sportsman, is pictured on a left page, and various charts showing performance of Turner Broadcasting System, Inc. are shown on the opposite page. Kurt Vonnegut, the novelist, is shown opposite a manuscript of one of his novels composed on a word processor. Maya Lin, an architecture student, is pictured opposite a perspective study of a spiral staircase.

Some facts on the annual reports published by companies:

- The report is usually issued in the spring.

- Nearly 10,000 companies produce annual reports.

- The average annual report is about 45 pages long, and the size seems to seems to be increasing each year.

- Companies spend from $2.00 to $8.00 a copy for their reports.

- Many companies have outside firms design and prepare their annual reports.

- The annual report is used to express the company's philosophy and is seen as being in competition with other companies' annual reports.

Ideas for School District's Annual Reports

What lessons can school administrators learn from the annual reports of the best-run companies?

First, do not be reluctant to allocate the resources necessary to produce a quality report that is well thought out, well produced, and well disseminated. This

117

means that school superintendents must be willing to hire outside marketing and public relations specialists to design and produce the report if competent personnel are not available in the school district. School superintendents must understand that some conservative members of the community may "revolt" against spending the money to produce a quality annual report. However, other community members will feel proud, not only of the quality of efforts made in the school district, but also of the quality of the report. School administrators should no longer be satisfied to produce a poorly developed and poorly printed report about the progress of the school district. Excellence in education should not be confined to the academic program, but should be spread throughout all areas and activities of the school district. A quality effort to portray what the school district is accomplishing in their quest for excellence in the form of an attractive and well-conceived annual report, can be an important marketing tool for attracting parents to the schools, as well as retaining high-achieving students. Marketing of the school district through an annual report should be viewed as an important and serious endeavor.

Second, when designing the annual report, prepare the table of contents first. This information will act as a guide for the preparation of the annual report.

Third, establish a theme for the annual report. Some appropriate themes might be the following:

- A Passion for Excellence
- Fulfilling the Promise of Excellence
- The Process of Becoming Excellent
- Our Quest to Become the Best

How should the theme be established and by whom? It should be decided on several months before the start of the school year at a joint meeting of the superintendent team, school administrators, and supervisors. (Some educators may wish to include other people on the committee to decide the theme of the annual report. This is certainly acceptable. The reason I suggested the above group is because these are the people who will be responsible for perpetuating the essence of the theme throughout the school organization.)

Fourth, illustrate the annual report with charts, graphics, and photographs, to give emphasis to printed words. The old adage "A picture is worth a thousand words" still prevails today. In addition to the charts, graphics, and photographs scattered throughout the report to add visual interest, there should also be adequate white space so that the content is not cluttered.

Fifth, include at the beginning of the annual a message to the stakeholders, prepared jointly by the president of the schoolboard and the superintendent. The message should give the reader an understanding of what goals and objectives were set by the district, how well they were realized, and what the stakeholders should look for during the upcoming school year. Somewhere near the message to the stakeholders should be a list of highlights from the body of the report—for example:

- Median SAT scores rose from 547 to 575 in math and from 594 to 611 in verbal skills.

- Student attendance increased from 89.5 to 93.7 percent.

- The percentage of students entering college increased from 72 to 84 percent.

Sixth, include in the main body of the annual report several sections that summarize various activities, efforts, and programs energized to achieve excellence. The following are important topics that should be discussed in the main body of the annual report:

- Student Learning and Growth. This should be the largest section in the annual report. It should cover efforts made to improve student learning and growth, student academic achievements, and PSAT, SAT, and other test results. Some attention should be given to each of the academic areas. Also, student recognition and awards should be covered in this section.

- Human Resources. This section should list the number of professional and civil-service employees in the district, as well as salaries and related expenditures, number of employees hired, training efforts, awards received by school personnel, and promotions. Also included in this section should be absentee rates of school personnel and what this absenteeism cost the school district.

- Facilities. A description of any new or improved facilities should be given in this section. It is also a good policy to discuss the condition of present facilities that will need to be either improved or replaced.

- Management Information System. The school district's use of management information technology should be highlighted in this section. The community should be kept appraised of what efforts the school district is making to develop and extend computer applications in the management of the school district. The cost of computer operations should be shared with the reader, as well as a description of how the equipment is used and what the school district can hope to gain from the system.

- Research and Development. This section of the report should contain information on products researched and developed to enhance the learning process. These products could be designed to facilitate either the teaching process or the learning process.

- Goals and Objectives. Somewhere within the first sections of the annual report should be the citation of the school district's goals and objectives, as well as progress made in achieving them. All reports of performance should be substantiated, and any actions taken to improve performance should be explained.

- Programs. Each program should be explained in detail—its function, progress, and how students have benefited from it. Cost should also be included so that parents can see what they are getting for their money.

- Community Participation. The staff of an excellent school district realizes that the district's purpose is to serve students and the community in which they and their parents live. Therefore the annual report should contain information on programs and activities the school district initiated in an effort to establish a holistic relationship with the community.

- Auditors' Report. A statement from the auditors should be included attesting to the present financial position of the school district and signed by the auditor. This means that the audit of the financial records must begin in early May and end around the second week in July, so that the annual report can be submitted to stakeholders by the end of July.

- School Management Report. The integrity and objectivity of the information presented in the annual report should be certified to by both the president of the school board and the superintendent of schools. This certification should encompass two main categories—the accuracy of the information on student learning and growth and the accuracy of the financial report.

The following checklist contains specific types of information a school administrator might want to consider including in an annual report.

Financial Information

Financial highlights and summary	Taxes
	Capital expenditures
Investments	Income from operations
Value of plants	Grant awards
Operating statement	Explanatory notes and
Financial position	auditors' certificate
Future outlook	

Nonfinancial Information

Facts about the school district:	Employee benefits:
Brief history of school district:	Pension plan
Size, and location	Insurance

School district publications: Health and safety
    practices
Training and
    development

Facts about employees:

Number   Names of treasurer, attorney
Average age   and accountant
Length of service   Dates of important meetings
Thumbnail biographies   Future projects
Organizational chart   School wellness program
Wage increase

Year-to-Year Comparisons

Student achievements   Taxes
Cost to educate a student   Financial progress
SAT results   Research and
Physical education awards   development efforts
Teacher and student   Employee suggestions
  absenteeism   Employee statistics
School awards   New employees
Retirement and promotion

Strategies for Achieving Excellence

- Make a list of some unusual things to include in the annual report, such as:

  — The number of miles the superintendent and other central administrators have traveled throughout the school district practicing management by wandering around.

— Ridiculous rules that were eliminated in the school district.
— The best act of caring demonstrated by a school employee.
— Efforts made to give the school district a soul.
— The five best employee suggestions and their impact on the school district.
— Efforts made by the school district to reduce paperwork.
— Stories of the ways teams became winners, school champions excelled, or school people received awards or recognition.
— Strategies implemented by the superintendent to make the school more egalitarian.
— A description of what the school district has done to demonstrate that it respects its people.

• Obtain the annual reports of the companies discussed in this lesson and use one or more as models in developing your annual report. Contact a marketing expert in the community and ask him or her to review your annual report and give you suggestions for improving it.

• Select your most recent annual report and critique it on the basis of three criteria established by the American Management Association for evaluating the effectiveness of an annual report: interest, clearness, and completeness. Use the substance of this evaluation to improve your annual report.

• Lesson 9 •

Establish Circles of Excellence

As far as I'm concerned, it's the only way to operate
. . . there isn't any other way in today's world.
—F. James McDonald

In Achieving Excellence in Our Schools I described the need to provide teachers with autonomy in order to encourage intrapreneurship. To accomplish this, I recommended that the school be reorganized into permanent, involuntary teams. In this lesson I will show how voluntary teams can further the pursuit of excellence by solving problems and enhance school people's self-esteem. You are probably already familiar with quality circles, employee participation circles, action teams, job enrichment teams, employee communication circles, participation action circles, professional development teams, school improvement circles, or working groups. I used to refer to educational quality circles as school improvement circles, but today I use the term circles of excellence, because it suggests independent attempts by groups of people to initiate certain improvements in an effort to achieve excellence. Solving a problem, no matter how small, is one more step toward achieving excellence in our schools, and this is the overriding mission of circles of excellence.

125

Defining a Circle of Excellence

A circle of excellence is a team of 3 to 11 school people who work in similar grades, subject areas, or support services and who voluntarily meet on a weekly basis (usually one hour per week, on school time) to identify, select, and analyze and solve a problem and at times, implement the solution. Circle leaders and members are trained in various problem-solving techniques. Usually the principal is the initial circle leader. However, once a circle is operating smoothly, the members may select their own leader from among the circle membership.

Circles of excellence are based on certain motivational principles derived from the theories of McGregor, Maslow, and Herzberg. The idea is that people are more prone to perform at a high level when they are provided with responsibility, given an opportunity to achieve and be recognized for the achievement; they will be more creative and will experience a sense of self-fulfillment and an increase in personal dignity. Circles of excellence are based on two assumptions: (1) that the person performing a job is the real expert about the job and should be given the responsibility for solving job-related problems and (2) that when school administrators give this responsibility to their school people, they will respond to their jobs in a responsible manner.

Some of the advantages of the program are as follows:

- Participation in a circle of excellence provides opportunities for people to satisfy their emotional and motivational needs, such as the need for achievement, recognition, self-esteem, and self-actualization.

- Being circle members gives people a feeling of control over their jobs, thereby reducing any fears they may have concerning arbitrary use of power by the supervisor.

- Being a member of a circle of excellence is one of the most effective types of on-the-job training.

- The circle of excellence provides an opportunity to diminish status differentials between circle members and their supervisors, this unleashes the potential power of the group for improved decision-making and performance.

- Decision-making improves because of the number of alternatives, options, and ideas generated by circle members. Creative solutions to problems emerge through the collective wisdom of the group.

Blue-Collar vs. White-Collar Circles

When the quality circle concept was first introduced, it was used primarily for solving problems relating to the manufacturing of products. As a result of the success experienced by blue-collar employees, white-collar employees began to implement this problem-solving process. Today, a number of white-collar organizations, among them airlines, hospitals, banks, insurance companies, advertising agencies, public relations firms, and school districts, have adopted the quality circle concept. Although there are presently more blue-collar employees than white collar employees implementing the quality circle concept, it is likely that, in the future, the number of white-collar quality circles may exceed that of blue-collar quality circles.

The following comparative analysis demonstrates some basic differences between the traditional blue-collar circle and the type of white-collar circle that one would find in a school district.

Blue-Collar Circle	*White-Collar Circle*
• Circle members tend to be be motivated by a desire for recognition.	• Circle members tend to be be motivated by a desire for achievement
• Less nonverbal communication is likely to take place in circle meetings	• More nonverbal communication is likely to take place in circle meetings.
• Circle members tend to be goal oriented.	• Circle members tend to have more interpersonal problems.
• Circle members usually confine problem-solving to job content	• Circle members usually tackle problems related to both job content and job context.
• Circle members usually confront problems peculiar to their own work unit.	• Circle members are likely to attempt to solve problems related to other units.
• Circle members are less prone to cancel meetings; there are fewer circle meetings.	• Circle members are more prone to cancel meetings; there are more circle meeting problems.

- Circle members are more likely to analyze a problem from a statistical point of view.

- Circle members tend to have less of a statistical orientation. They are more apt to try to talk through the problem or exchange opinions about it.

Quality Circles of Two Companies

Each year more and more companies and even a few more school districts have have recognized the merits of the quality circle concept and have adopted it as one more approach toward excellence. The following is a brief account of two companies—one blue collar, the other white collar–that have used this people-solving and "people-building" process with much success. Westinghouse adopted the quality circle program in 1978, and within a year the concept had exploded throughout the company. In 1980, the company began an ownership plan whereby managers assumed direct supervision of specific quality circles. Facilitators were loaned to managers to assist them in the training and development of their circles. Westinghouse used the quality circle program as a way of moving toward participative management. First, it used quality circles to solve unit-related problems. These circles proved so successful that the company began establishing other kinds of quality circles, called participative teams, react teams, and option teams. The essential difference between the quality circles and the teams is that the teams worked on immediate problems and took less time to solve them. Participative teams consisted of a cross-section of people who tackled problems related to a specific project. React teams were essentially *ad hoc* committees that were organized to make an immediate decision in order to resolve some major difficulty. Option teams were organized to find ways to reduce inventory time. All members of circles and "quasi-circles" were trained in problem-solving techniques, communication, and group dynamics. Nearly 10,000 people are now involved in the Westinghouse Participative Management Programs that resulted from the quality circle concept. Since the inception of the program, $20 million has been saved and 400 management presentations have been conducted. Among the many benefits realized by Westinghouse people from these various types of quality circles are improved communication among all people, better understanding of the operations of the company, more self-confidence on the part of company people, improved teamwork and team building, and improved training and development of people.

Security Pacific Corporation initiated seven pilot quality circles in 1982. During that year one circle saved Security Pacific $75,000. At the end of 1982, management sanctioned the program. Security Pacific now has 72 quality circles, of which 51 are active. (Because the program is voluntary, some circles become inactive for one reason or another—for example, because of summer vacation. Eventually some of these inactive circles become reactivated.) Two unique features of Security Pacific's quality circle program are the absence of a steering committee to govern the program and the absence of management participation. Facilitators and leaders meet once a month to update everyone on the disposition of quality circle projects. Recently a quality circle worked on a project that will save the bank $500,000. One quality circle discovered that instituting a certain form would save the bank $50,000. Another circle recommended the reuse of a card in processing credit applications, a move that is projected to result in considerable savings. On the "people side" of the ledger, bank employees who participated in the quality circle program have profited in several ways. For example, employees learned analytical skills and many of them realized for the first time their real power and authority to solve problems. Many of the circle members maintain that they are now able to see "the whole problem," and some circle members indicate that they are able to view problems within the organization from a management prospective.

Problems Solved by Circles

Circles usually spend a large percentage of their time solving problems that affect performance. After they have been in existence for a while and have matured, circles may tackle more complex and larger problems. In a school district, quality circles often are successful in solving problems that have been neglected by the administration because of lack of time, problems that administration is not aware of, or administration believes cannot be solved. Depending on the district, these problems may number in the hundreds or even thousands. A problem can be classified as one of three types:

- Type 1—those over which circle members have direct control, because they relate to the individual working unit represented by the quality circle.

- Type 2—those over which circle members have limited and indirect control. The influence of central administrator is required to implement solutions to such problems. Although some of the problems involve job context factors, most deal with job content factors, such as policy and administration, supervision, working conditions, and interpersonal relations. Type 2 problems involve one or more units that have similar or common concerns.

- Type 3—those over which central administrators have direct control. Such problems usually involve job content factors such as achievement, recognition, the work itself, responsibility, advancement, and growth. Type 3 problems tend to be related to the school district as a whole; that is, they are problems that affect all units. I highly recommend that when the circle of excellence program is initially implemented, circle members focus their attention on Type 1 problems. Once the program has had an opportunity to "thaw out," Type 2 problems can be tackled.

The problems that circles of excellence work on initially should take no more than two months to solve. As circles begin to solve Type 2 problems, more time will be needed. However, even most complex problems should be solved within three to six months.

In an effort not to encroach on the territory of unions, the steering committee that oversees the circle of excellence program should identify, and describe in the program's charter problems that the circle will not address. Although these problems will vary from one organization to another, the following appear to be areas to avoid:

- Wages and salaries
- Fringe benefits
- Disciplinary policies
- Employment policies
- Termination policies
- Grievances
- Collective bargaining items
- Design of new products
- Sales and marketing policies
- Personality conflicts

Hybrid Circles of Excellence

A number of "hybrid" circles have been created that have, to some degree, strengthened the usefulness of the circle of excellence in solving, simple, and complex problems. Each hybrid is explained below.

Joint Circle. When the circle of excellence program has begun to prove its worth and many Type 1 problems have been solved, the facilitator should arrange to have two circles from different units come together, either on a temporary basis to solve a common Type 2 problem, or on a permanent basis to share information on problem-solving activities. Usually, when a joint quality circle has solved a problem, the group is disbanded until the facilitator or circle leader feels that formation of another joint circle of excellence is desirable because of a common concern. For example, a joint circle of excellence from the intermediate school and the junior high school might meet to solve articulation and coordination problems.

Administration Circles. Administration circles consist of school administrators of similar units; they usually meet to share information on the activities of their quality circles or to solve Type 2 problems. Although administration circles have been slow to emerge in most U.S. organizations, there has been some recent interest generated by the International Association of Quality Circles.

Administration Teams. Administration teams consist of administrators from different levels of the school organization, who meet as a group to solve Type 3 problems, after which the teams are disbanded. When more organizations realize that basic and advanced problem-solving techniques are useful for solving major or complex organizational problems, more of them will adopt administration teams.

The purposes of a circle of excellence will vary from school district to school district, depending on the unique needs of each district. One method for assessing the circle of excellence program is to evaluate the extent to which purposes are being achieved. Most circle programs have the following purposes:

- To encourage a spirit of teamwork.

- To tap the gold mine of unused skills, abilities, and talents of school people.

- To create an environment that is conducive to open communication and mutual trust among school people.

- To enrich the job of school people by giving them

the opportunity to share power and authority with administrators.

- To unleash the ideas of school people for solving job-related problems.

- To create opportunities for school people to work together and to participate in improving their job situation.

- To improve morale and job satisfaction.

- To provide opportunities for professional and personal growth.

- To foster an attitude of problem prevention.

- To provide school people with the opportunity to receive recognition from administration for solving problems.

- To improve the quality of teaching and services.

- To effect cost savings through on-the-job improvements.

Basic Elements of Circles

The school board, the administrators, the steering committee, the facilitators, and the circle members all perform a vital role in making circles work. The school board and school administrators at all levels must provide support if the circle of excellence program is to be successful. These people must demonstrate their commitment to the quality circle concept by becoming knowledgeable about the program, by visiting the various quality circles, and by disseminating written documents to school and community people espousing the merits of the circle of excellence program.

The steering committee is usually composed of various administrators from different levels of the school organization. The steering committee is responsible for developing the charter governing the operations of circles of excellence, selecting a facilitator, establishing long and short range plans to guide the efforts of the quality circle program, establishing a budget to accommodate the circle of excellence activities, determining the form of recognition to give to circle members, and doing whatever else is necessary to make a quality circle program successful. Steering committee members can demonstrate support for the circle of excellence program by attending circle meetings, management presentations, and the annual circle of excellence conference.

The facilitator is a member of the steering committee and is responsible for directing the activities of this governing body. Though not a member of the circle of excellence, the facilitator is responsible for the operations of the circle program and should actively help the circle leader to operate an effective and smooth meeting. The facilitator—the person most knowledgeable about the program—must act as a resource person, a trainer, a coordinator, a promoter, and a problem-solver, as well as filling a host of other roles needed to ensure the success of the program. Part of the job of the facilitator is to maintain support for the circles through a campaign to keep administrators informed by such means as awareness sessions, newsletters, and invitations to visit circle of excellence functions.

The circle leader is usually the immediate supervisor of circle members (in education, this person would be the principal), although in some instances other circle members have been known to assume the position of leader. The leader conducts the circle meetings and orchestrates all of the activities that make the circle of excellence work.

The core of the circle of excellence is its members, volunteers who perform basically the same type of day-to-day work and who generally report to the same supervisor. They are trained in basic and advanced problem-solving techniques and in group dynamics.

Circle members do not have all the answers to the problems of the school district; from time to time they need specialists and experts to assist them in defining and analyzing problems. Sometimes outside consultants may be necessary, especially when Type 2 and 3 problems are being addressed.

Although all school people are given opportunities to volunteer to serve on circles of excellence, some do not because of a host of reasons. Nonmembers should, however, be thought of as an important resource of the school district and should be involved in the circle of excellence activities as much as possible. People within the school district should be seen as a cadre of specialists within particular, identifiable skills which can be used to shed light on problems. Circle members should not be reluctant to contact an expert from any area, as long as that person can be of service to them in the analysis and solution of a problem. One caution: Sometimes, an individual called upon to assist in the analysis of a problem may want to take over the problem and to insist that circle members accept his or her perceptions of its real cause(s). It is the circle leader's responsibility to see to it that this doesn't take place; once the expert has fulfilled to his or her charge, that person should leave the circle of excellence meeting.

From time to time nonmembers should be brought up to date on the progress being made by the circle of excellence program. Circle members should also strive continually to get nonmembers to join circles of excellence.

Phases of Circles

There are several phases in the operation of a circle of excellence, which must be viewed as part of a comprehensive and systematic process. If one or more phases are omitted or improperly executed, program results are likely to be disappointing.

Phase I—Identifying problems. Circle members use brainstorming to identify a large number and variety of problems, from which they will choose a single problem to work on. Although circle members select their own problem, nonmembers should be encouraged to assist in the identification of problems.

Phase II—Selecting a problem. Circle members may go through two or three rounds of discussion before they select a specific problem to solve. During the initial brainstorming session, Type 1 problems should receive preference because addressing one of the relatively simple Type problems will allow circle members to experience some quick success and to gain some experience with the process.

Phase III—Gathering data on the problem. Circle members are responsible for gathering data and information about the problem. Usually data collection will involve the study of reports, computer printouts, checklists, research data, information from specialists and experts, and drawings. Information that is collected during this phase should enable circle members to develop various displays to help illuminate the magnitude of the problem.

Phase IV—Analyzing the data. The assembled data should be organized into histograms, scattergrams, graphs, pareto charts, control charts, or other graphic displays that can help point up specific reasons for the problem.

Phase V—Solving the problem. Circle members generate ideas as to how the problem can be solved and then select the most appropriate solution. Some techniques that may be used during this phase are function analysis, force-field analysis, and cause-and-effect diagrams. Function analysis is used to determine an improved method for performing a task or process. Force-field analysis is used to determine whether to use a driving force or a restraining force to solve the problem. A cause-and-effect diagram helps circle members to identify the possible causes of the problem and to arrive at a solution.

Phase VI—Verifying the solution. Circle members verify the proposed solution by conferring with specialists and experts or referring to some other source.

Phase VII—Presenting the proposed solution to administration. Once a proposal for a solution has been arrived at by the circle of excellence, arrangements are made by the facilitator or circle leader for circle members to present their proposal to a group of administrators for review and approval. The solution to the problem should be presented to the administration both orally and in writing. The presentation of the proposal can be one of the most exciting phase of the problem-solving process, and it should be executed with care. An agenda should be prepared to guide the activities of the meeting. The presentation should be rehearsed until the circle members, as a group, are ready to give a command performance. A question-and-answer session, as well as a status report concerning the next circle project, should be included on the meeting agenda.

Phase VIII—Rendering a decision. Usually administration is ready to make a decision regarding the proposed solution at the conclusion of the presentation. This decision might be to approve the proposal, to reject it, or to withhold a decision until further information is forthcoming. My experience indicates that about 80 percent of the proposed solutions are approved by school administrators at the presentation. When a proposed solution is rejected, it is often because implementing the solution would cost large sums of money. At times, a circle of excellence may not get immediate approval because additional information is needed, or because the matter must be discussed with someone within or outside of the school organization. This is particularly likely if another school district has implemented the solution proposed by the circle of excellence. Sometimes the circle of excellence must be prepared to come up with an alternative solution. In any event, administration should render a decision about the proposed solution within a reasonable period of time.

Phase IX—Implementing the solution. Whenever possible, the circle of excellence should develop an action plan to implement the solution to the problem. If this is not feasible, the circle of excellence should monitor the actions of the individual or group responsible for implementing the solution. Periodically, program reports should be presented to all school people. Circle members must understand that it is not enough to suggest a solution to a problem—the solution must also be implemented.

Potential Pitfalls

Once a circle of excellence has been given the opportunity to select a problem, the group should be provided with the time and resources needed to analyze the problem. There are three potential pitfalls in the operation of a quality circle program:

- Administrators may give lip service to the quality circle program but remain reluctant to share power and authority with people in the district. Many human beings are addicted to power; once they assume it they are reluctant to surrender it to anyone, particularly those below them in the school district hierarchy. These same administrators may either try to solve the problem themselves or intentionally withhold information from circle members so that they fail in their attempt to do so.

- Older school people may be reluctant to analyze and to solve problems, primarily because they are used to the subservient role they have always played within the school organization. They may not feel right doing what administrators have always done or were supposed to do. This traditional view of work limits their acceptance of participatory management and inhibits their ability to share power and authority with administrators.

- At times, circle leaders have been known to solve problems that have been identified by the circle of excellence without properly involving circle members in the analysis of the problem. This attitude is a real threat to the quality circle concept for two reasons. First, the solution to the problem may not

141

be what the circle members would have arrived at collectively. By not using the collective experience, skills, talents, and abilities of circle members to analyze and solve the problems, the circle precludes the possibility that circle members might have arrived at a different explanation of the problem and a better or less expensive solution. Second, the circle leader who bypasses circle members in this way is denying them two powerful motivators—achievement and recognition. One of the most important rationales for the quality circle concept is "people building," or organizational development. When the analysis of a problem is assumed entirely by the circle leader, the real intent of the program is not being achieved. The circle leader must understand that he or she cannot ever have all of the answers to problems. An effective circle leader does not need to solve problems; rather it is the leader's job to see to it that problems are solved by the entire group.

The circle of excellence program is a proven process for introducing change and improving the quality of services or products. Organizations that adhere to the established procedures for planning, implementing, maintaining, evaluating, and improving the circle of excellence program will reap high rewards in job satisfaction, cost savings, increased productivity, improved quality of work life, better morale, and a host of other benefits. In all cases, where the program has failed to produce the expected results, the limitations of the participants were solely responsible for the failure. To reduce the probability of failure, the following criteria should be adhered to in implementing the circle of excellence program:

- Membership in a circle of excellence should be limited to 11 people.
- Participation in the program should be voluntary.
- Circle members should be allowed to choose their own problems, analyze them, propose a solution, and if possible, implement the solution.
- Circle of excellence meetings should be held on a workday, or circle members should be paid for their time when meetings take place after the workday.
- The facilitator should be carefully selected.
- Facilitators and circle leaders should receive training in problem-solving techniques, communication, and group dynamics and motivation; all school people should receive awareness training in the quality circle concept.
- The facilitator should attend circle of excellence meetings until circle members are able to function effectively by themselves, and then should be phased out of the meetings.
- Administration should respond to proposed solutions in a timely manner.
- Circle members should be recognized by administration for their problem-solving efforts.
- The circle of excellence program should be initiated on a pilot basis first, and then expanded through

out the school district after adjustments have been made to minimize problems.

Strategies for Achieving Excellence

- Select an assistant superintendent to become trained as a circle of excellence facilitator. This person should be be charged with the responsibility of managing the program in your district.

- Become a member of the National Association for Quality Circles. With this membership, you can get a list of profit and nonprofit organizations that have established quality circle programs. Contact some of these organizations and ask them to share their quality circle materials with you. Also contact the Association for Supervision and Curriculum Development. This organization should be able to put you in touch with school districts that have implemented quality circles. ASCD also has a videotape entitled "Quality Circles: Problem Solving Tool for Educators" ($225 for ASCD members, $260 nonmembers) that shows how quality circles can solve school-related problems.

- Design a circle of excellence pilot program, and meet with the superintendent and the school board to discuss and get approval for the program. Divide the plan into five phases: preliminary, training, installation, maturation, and evaluation.

- Make provisions for several principals, teachers. union representatives, and the superintendent to attend the annual conference of the National Association of Quality Circles and to visit two or three school districts that have implemented the quality circle concept.

- Using the materials collected from other organizations and school districts, prepare a Steering Committee Charter, a Circle of Excellence Charter, and an Award and Recognition Plan.

- Conduct workshops to familiarize all school people with the quality circle concept. Invite participants to become circle of excellence members.

- Select schools that will participate in the pilot program; train principals and assistant principals to become circle members.

- Prepare necessary written materials and obtain appropriate audiovisual aids to conduct the training.

- Evaluate the pilot program and give the reports to the superintendent and the school board, to obtain a decision as to whether the circle of excellence program will be continued.

- Train additional circle of excellence facilitators, and expand the circle of excellence program throughout the district.

Create an Atmosphere of Caring, Intimacy, and Trust

> If the people around you are spiteful and callous and will not hear you, fall down before them and beg their forgiveness, for in truth you are to blame for their not wanting to hear you.
>
> —William Whyte

How do school administrators compare to managers of the best-run companies in the extent to which they care for, are intimate with and trust their people? Not very favorably. Let's consider the way some very similar situations were handled by a school district and by one of the best-run companies.

When the director of pupil personnel of a suburban school district, after having served the school well for more than ten years, suddenly suffered a stroke, he was allowed to use up his sick days. But soon after these were used, the superintendent applied such pressure that the personnel director was forced to resign. When a 27-year-old IBM employee had a stroke after only about a year on the job, IBM allowed the stricken individual to receive his salary for one year, way beyond his accumulated sick

147

days. After the year was up, the company hired the former employee's wife so that the family's income could continue without an interruption.

When the director of urban education of a medium-sized school district woke up with an infected fever blister on her lip and a swollen right jaw, she came in to work anyway because it was the day the superintendent's cabinet was to meet to discuss school affairs. Did the superintendent recognize the dedication of the distraught and ailing director and suggest that she go home and recuperate? She did not. When an employee of 3M developed an ailment that she claimed was minor, 3M's CEO urged her to take his own car so that she could go home to recuperate.

In 1984, the superintendent of a small northeastern school district was asked to put a lounge in the women's restroom. He said that none was available for the men's restroom and that he didn't feel that one was needed in the women's rest room. In contrast, back in 1929 an employee suggestion box at Hallmark included a suggestion that "space be allotted and fixed up that can be used as a restroom for women who are sick. We do not want a recreation center—merely a place to rest when needed." In 1930, a medical room with a graduate nurse in charge was established at Hallmark. Medical care has been available at the company ever since, along with comfort facilities far beyond that suggested by the person submitting the suggestion.

A prevailing problem among school bus drivers is that the tedious driving without power steering and the uncomfortable seats have produced back problems, some so serious that frequent visits to a doctor or chiropractor have become routine. When a similar problem was identified by the drivers for Publix Super Markets, the company installed special orthopedic seats to improve the drivers' posture, thereby reducing the likelihood of back troubles.

I certainly don't want to imply with these examples that all superintendents of schools are uncaring. But school administrators must pay more attention to the human values of caring, trust and intimacy if school districts are to achieve excellence.

Caring

Caring is one humanistic value that needs more emphasis in our school districts. Caring is exhibited when an individual or group shares or sacrifices a resource for the benefit of another person or group. A resource could be money, time, energy, power, or information. If the resource that is shared is of value and sharing it causes the sharer some hardship, then the act of sharing is an example of caring through sacrificing. Obviously, the greatest form of caring is caring through sacrificing. A pure form of sacrificing is when the individual or group receives only internal gratification for the act—that is when the sacrifice remains anonymous. The most extreme example of caring through sacrifice is when a person who is starving gives up his or her food without recognition so that another may not starve.

Tom Peters and Nancy Austin report that "zest and enthusiasm and really caring mark all the companies we've looked at." The managers of the best-run companies work hard to establish an atmosphere in which employees feel important and cared for, and they go out of their way to put their principles into practice. Managers in these companies realize that it makes good sense to take care of their greatest asset, their people. They know that caring is reciprocal; it usually brings in a return greater than the investment.

At Quad/Graphics concern for their employees is expressed this way: "Our emphasis is not on the numbers but rather on people who are caring and sharing in common values and attitudes, people who have stretched their minds and broadened their horizons to bring printing from the craft of the Middle Ages to the technology of the Space Age; and people—ordinary people—who have achieved this extraordinary result through the Quad philosophy of people helping people to become something more than they ever hoped to be."

At Hallmark concern for employees is embodied in a benefit package that includes short-term interest-free loans to meet emergencies; adoption assistance for those desiring to adopt a child; an employee-assistance program for individuals with alcohol or other problems; an employee-ownership plan that enables employees to own a part of the company; discounts on Hallmark's products; and physical-fitness facilities for employees desiring to keep themselves in shape.

Hewlett-Packard demonstrates that it cares for its people by maintaining a safe work environment and by consistently sharing with employees the responsibilities for defining and meeting goals, ownership of the company through stock-purchase plans, profits, and opportunities for personal and professional development, as well as burdens created by an economic crisis.

When Delta Air Lines was suffering large financial losses as a result of an economic crisis brought on by an oil embargo, deregulation, and a stagnant national economy, the company showed that it cared about its employees by rotating pilots and other people to other jobs and giving across-the-board increases in salary instead of laying off employees as other airlines were doing. These were indeed sacrifices on Delta's part, and they did not go unreciprocated. Shortly after Delta had weathered its crisis, the employees bought a $30 million jet to thank management for the caring way they had been treated.

Mary Kay demonstrates personally that she cares for her people by sending to each employee on her birthday a birthday card and a voucher for a free lunch for two. During Secretary's Week, all secretaries at Mary Kay Cosmetics get flowers and a coffee mug. When individuals are hired, each one gets an opportunity to meet personally with Mary Kay, who makes a point to visit training classes and to display pictures of employees rather than products in the company's headquarters.

A visit to any of the best-run companies reveals that employees are really cared for by management, and the employees are delighted to share the news with visitors:

"He makes me feel like we are part of his success."

"The bottom line here is people."

"They didn't have to do that."

"I enjoy coming to work here because the people here care."

"There is a spirit of camaraderie here that is unbelievable."

"The other day, my child got sick at school and the president gave me the use of his car to pick him up."

"There is a spirit of sharing here that you won't observe in other companies."

Intimacy

Intimacy is the second humanistic value that school administrators must emphasize if our schools are to achieve excellence. Intimacy is the product of a personal and earnest relationship that can only be established through the initiation of frequent social contacts, the nurturing of mutual trust, and the maintenance of security and goodwill.

When a manager starts to build an intimate relationship with his or her people, each party begins to measure the trustworthiness, personality and other factors that, to some degree, will emerge between them. This period of judging each other's worth is an essential part of building a foundation on which trust can be established.

Intimacy can be built in many ways. For example, in order to be more intimate with company people, Trammell Crow of Trammell Crow Company does not use a private office; he shares a large open space with other employees. He believes that in order to become intimate, people must be able to communicate without the barrier of a private office, and his employees cannot know that he cares for them if they cannot see him. At Northwestern Mutual Life Insurance Company, intimacy is nurtured in the job environment by creating a family atmosphere: all employees eat a free lunch in the same cafeteria, everybody is on a first-name basis, and flextime is used for the convenience of the "other family." Kollmorgen Corporation allocates $25,000 annually to a committee comprised of a cross section of company people that organizes social events for both employees and managers. Many of the funds have been used to sponsor outings at which all members of the organization and their families can mix. The rationale for the funds is that those who work together should play together. The comments of employees of these companies reflect their appreciation of the intimacy that is being nurtured in the workplace:

"You see the top people all the time. They work with you."

"Everybody here is on a first-name basis."

"We tend to socialize with each other after work; sometimes the president may join us."

"Do you know that when I first came to work here, Mary Kay invited me to her fabulous home? I felt really important."

"One day a year, all the top managers, including the president, come down into the plant and work on the assembly line with us. It's a fun day for all of us."

"This is an open place here."

"Do you know that the president visited my sick mother-in-law? He also sent her some flowers."

In order to become intimate with school people, school administrators must view them with equals and socialize with them on and off the job. Typical of the comments I have heard across the country is one voiced by an assistant commissioner of education, who said, "I don't believe in including my staff in my social life." If public education is ever to break down the barriers that presently exist between administrators and teachers, the former must become more sensitive to people. A primary way to become more sensitive is to make sure there is a continuous communication among all those in the district.

Most of the best-run companies maintain an open-door policy, not only psychologically but physically. An open door says in effect, "Come in and discuss your problems with me, whether it is job-related or personal." I have yet to encounter an open-door policy in a school district, although I have been told that some school districts in the West are moving in this direction. I applaud them, and I maintain that such a move is necessary in order for school districts to begin establishing an intimate relationship with school people. One cannot become intimate with another human being unless there is considerable communication.

In some large urban school districts, neither teachers nor students ever get to see the superintendent, and central administrators. Support personnel do not visit schools as often as they should. If the CEOs of some of the best-run companies can travel two hundred thousand miles each year to visit their divisions, plants and stores, surely school superintendents should be able to travel, in many instances less than a hundred miles to meet with school personnel, students, and parents.

Trust

Trust is the third most important humanistic value that school administrators must nurture. Trust is the confidence in the character, abilities, and truthfulness of a person that leads one to expect that the person's behavior will always be responsible and supportive of others. When trust exists in a school district, people can be confident that (1) information shared between two or more persons will not be used to harm either party; (2) words, promises, and agreements between parties can be depended upon; and (3) neither the person nor the property of either party will be violated.

Do some school districts demonstrate that they trust their people? Perhaps some do, but many do not. Establishing a trusting atmosphere is an explicit goal in the best-run companies. For example, the Borg-Warner phi-

losophy is that "we believe in the dignity of the individual. . . For Borg-Warner to succeed we must operate in a
climate of openness and trust." At Apple Computer it is
expected that "Employees should be able to trust the
motives and integrity of their superiors." The Dayton-
Hudson Corporation describes as one of its corporate
purposes, ". . . to provide an atmosphere which encourages employees' initiative and input and which fosters
trust, creativity, and economic security."

On the other hand, in my 25 years in public education, I have yet to read a single statement of a school
district's philosophy that mentions the word "trust."
Even the statement of Brookline High School, which
Peters and Austin include as a model in their book, *A
Passion for Excellence*, omits any reference to this humanistic value. To cite a concrete example of the lack of
trust in our school districts: each morning a time clock
reminds 57,000 New York City teachers and thousands
of teachers and other school personnel throughout the
country that neither the school board nor the superintendent trusts them to report and to leave school on time.
The best-run companies, such as Celestial Seasoning,
Donnelly Mirrors, and Moore, Inc. have long ago aban-
doned time clocks.

One way to establish a trusting atmosphere in an
organization is to involve as many people as possible in
the decision-making process, as the best-run companies
do. In fact, in many of these companies decisions are
made by consensus so that all people who will be affected
by decisions can participate in making them. Companies
such as Kollmorgen, Procter & Gamble, and Trammell
Crow are only a few that attempt to maximize the
number of people involved in the decision-making process. Although a few school districts are attempting to

implement management by consensus, much more must be done in this area. I firmly believe that trust will occur only when organizations begin to adopt consensus as a dominant strategy for arriving at decisions.

One of the ultimate expressions of trust is when an organization adopts either individual or team self-management. People-sensitive organizations such as Hewlett-Packard, People Express, Donnelly Mirrors, and Electro-Scientific are only a few of the companies that allow their people a great deal of latitude in making decisions and doing what must be done to achieve results. In contrast, most school districts rely mainly on hierarchical controls to get things done. Such a structure seldom creates a trusting atmosphere. Trust has long been an important humanistic value for the managers of Procter & Gamble. At this company, "people trust each other, and this material trust pervades everything we do. We trust each other to be truthful. When a recommendation comes forward, when a forecast is made, when data are analyzed, when a future action is promised, we accept the promises, the conclusions, the estimates, because we know that we don't deliberately mislead each other or try to hide the truth from each other."

3M demonstrates a high degree of trust by allowing its research scientists to spend 15 percent of their time in unassigned personal research pursuits. In this way scientist are allowed freedom on the job to create, experiment, or merely reflect on personal projects that one day in the future may benefit the company.

Trust is such an essential element at Quad/Graphics that the company formulated a document entitled "Trust in Trust at Quad/Graphics" which describes the company's philosophy:

- The Trust of Teamwork. Employees trust that together they will do better than as individuals apart.

- The Trust of Responsibility. Employees trust that each will carry his or her fair share of the load.

- The Trust of Productivity. Customers trust that work will be produced to the most competitive levels of pricing, quality and innovation.

- The Trust of Management. Shareholders, customers and employees trust that the company will make decisive judgments for the long-term rather than the short-term goals of today's profit.

- The Trust of Think-Small. We trust in each other. We regard each other as persons of equal rank; we respect the dignity of the individual by recognizing not only the individual's accomplishments, but the feelings and needs of the individual and family as well; and we all share the same goals and purposes in life.

The comments of employees of the best-run companies reveal the atmosphere of trust that has been carefully established:

"We don't have any rules here."

"We are given a lot of freedom and responsibilities here, and we love it."

"A mistake here is everybody's mistake."

"No one will tell you how to do your job."

"If egalitarianism means being cared for, being trusted, then this is an egalitarian organization."

Focusing on the Humanistic Values in the School District

Now that we have looked at some examples of how the best-run companies care for, are intimate with, and trust their people, let me discuss an approach that may help school administrators learn to focus more on these humanistic values of caring, intimacy and trust, and thus become more responsive to the needs of school people. I suggest that school administrators emulate a practice that originated with the Marriott Corporation during the 1930s, a practice that some people believe is responsible for the company's success. Each year all managers at Marriott are required to sign a pledge entitled "A Pledge for 198X; A Rededication to Excellence in Leadership." The document consists of a list of ten promises that each manager makes to his or her team/members. The first promise is "to set the right example for them by my own actions in all things." The second promise is "to be consistent in my temperament so that they know how to 'read' me and what to expect from me." A review of the pledge reveals that each statement is in reality a philosophy in itself.

The approach used at Marriott is a relatively simple way to foster attention to human values and the personal side of the activities within a school district. The district that develops its own "pledge of excellence" should do so carefully, so that the pledge becomes not simply a piece of paper but a "living document" that is taken to heart by school administrators. To ensure that this happens, this approach should be carried out in several steps.

The first step is to decide how the pledge is to be written. Will it be written by the superintendent to expose his or her management philosophy? Will it be prepared by the central administration team to reveal their shared views on the expected behavior of the administrator? Will it be a cross section of school administrators and teachers? Once this decision has been made, a first draft of the pledge statement should be written. After the draft has been thoroughly discussed by multiple committees of school administrators, the second draft should be prepared. The second draft can then be discussed by several small committees of school personnel. The separate recommendations of each committee should be recorded and used to arrive at a final document, one in which the input of all school people has been included.

The second step is for the training director and his or her staff to use the final version of the pledge to prepare a comprehensive training and development program that will show administrators how they can upgrade their effectiveness by adhering to the promises in the pledge. I strongly recommend that instead of attempting to perform the training in one swoop, the training director conduct a series of twenty 15-minute sessions, one per week, with two or three sessions devoted to each promise. This type of long-term training will help to inculcate a strong culture based on the pledge statement. No one should ever expect to improve a culture within a short period of time.

The third step is to give a copy of the pledge to all school people and have supervisors discuss it with them. All school personnel should understand that they will be involved in assessing the extent to which their supervisor carries out the pledge statement. The discussion should clearly identify what will be done to improve school administrators' behavior in areas in need of improvement.

The fourth step should take place three months after the training program has concluded. An assessment should be prepared to determine the extent to which each administrator is meeting each promise. The instrument should be administered to each school administrator, and the results should be analyzed and discussed with each one.

The final step in the process is to have each school administrator prepare a professional improvement plan in which promises needing improvement are identified, activities to improve those areas are defined, and performance standards are indicated. Administrators' performance on the professional improvement plan should be assessed on a bi-weekly basis.

Another method of developing a pledge statement is to have each school administrator prepare his or her own pledge statement based on needs mutually agreed upon with the superintendent. At the end of a predetermined period of time, all school people within the school unit are asked to evaluate how well the school administrator has lived up to his or her pledges. This evaluation is then used as a basis for the superintendent in determining tactics for improving those areas that have been pinpointed for improvement.

The inculcation of a strong culture of caring, intimacy, and trust throughout the entire school district is the most effective way to ensure that school administrators treat people with kindness and compassion. But the inculcation of a strong culture is an ongoing process; it may take a long time before these values permeate the entire district. The "pledge of excellence" approach that I have described can be used in the short term to make sure there is noticeable improvement in the manner in which school administrators treat their people.

STRATEGIES FOR ACHIEVING EXCELLENCE

- Limit the use of job description and organizational charts.
- Perpetuate a "What's good for school administrators is good for teachers" policy.
- Permit spouses to attend orientation meetings.
- Sponsor at least four social activities during the school year.
- Start athletic teams and join in with teachers and other school people.
- Celebrate employees' birthdays.
- Always keep your word.
- Share and equalize power with teachers.
- Permit the use of flexible time at the beginning and ending of the school day.
- Remove time clocks.
- Permit school people to speak out about a bad school policy.
- Institute an open-door policy.
- Reach decisions by consensus.
- Reduce organizational levels.
- Visit sick employees.
- Call all school people by their first names.

- Avoid separation of school people by titles, status or position.

- Invite school people to your house.

- Promote from within.

- Provide early release for school people during summer months.

- Provide quiet rooms where school people can release tension.

- Share timely information freely with school people.

- Hire handicapped people.

- Establish a cradle-to-grave approach to school administration.

- Use open space partitions.

- Establish small units (teams).

- Institute "management by wandering around."

Manage by Wandering Around

Managers have a direct responsibility for employees'
training, performance, and general well-being. To
carry out this responsibility, managers must move
around to find out how people feel about their jobs
and what they think will make their work more
productive and meaningful.
— David Packard and William R. Hewlett

In their book *A Passion for Excellence*, Tom Peters
and Nancy Austin report in dismay the claim of a county
school superintendent that there would be some painful
consequences from the school board if he were to begin
wandering around the school district. I do not believe
this represents the sentiment of the majority of boards of
education. Most boards give their superintendent complete freedom to meet as frequently as possible with
school people. One of the roles of the superintendent is to
keep the board informed of new principles and practices
in managing people, and the school administrator who
does not wander around the district cannot be performing this role effectively.

Far too many school superintendents and administrators do not make efforts to meet with people throughout
the district. This happens for one (or more) reasons.
First, they have become accustomed to managing the

school district in the traditional way, using their offices as command posts. Second, many school administrators have failed to develop a self-managed central administration team, and as a result team administrative members must constantly be told what to do and how to do it. Third, some administrators are lazy and don't want to put forth the extra effort to get out of their seats and meet with people. Fourth, many school administrators either don't plan or are poor planners; thus they engage in reactive management or crisis management, which leaves them exhausted and with little time to become people-sensitive managers.

Fortunately a growing number of superintendents and other school administrators are being influenced by books *In Search of Excellence* and *A Passion for Excellence*, and are starting to meet with school and community people on a frequent basis. In some places school board members have joined in the management-by-walking-around parade. Even William Bennett, Secretary of the United States Department of Education has been practicing management by walking around, by visiting and teaching in high schools around the nation. I hope he doesn't stop. In fact, I think it would be great if he would encourage his administrative team to do some wandering around from time to time. Bill Bennett and his top-level administrators could serve as excellent role models for all school administrators. Keep wandering around, Bill.

Wandering Is not Rambling

Rambling is not the same as wandering. When a person rambles, he or she walks around without having a specific goal in mind. In contrast, there are goals to management by wandering around, the most important of which is to keep in touch with people and to address their concerns. Sometimes a school administrator may intend to manage by wandering around but actually ends up simply rambling.

The administrator who is simply rambling around the school ends up in aimless chit-chat; true management by wandering around is a systematic process that involves seeking out people to connect with, actively listening to them, facilitating their conversation, and following through on their concerns. The administrator who is merely rambling usually fails to carry out the last step of following through, whereas true management by wandering around is not a complete process until action is promised and carried through within a reasonable time span. The administrator who merely rambles ends up talking mainly to teachers and other administrators; true management by wandering around involves meeting with all types of people during the course of a school year. Mere rambling will not necessarily contribute to a thorough grasp of details about the school district. Management by wandering around, because it is systematic, will help administrators stay well informed. Finally, mere rambling around the district will not necessarily contribute to an atmosphere of caring and trust—on the contrary, it may make people feel as though they are being "spied on." But true management by wandering around will help nurture a caring and intimate relationship among all the people in the district, because it is systematic, because its purpose is to allow people to express themselves openly, and because it is not mere conversation but action as well.

What Is Management by Wandering Around?

Management by wandering around is a practice by which central administrators make frequent informal contact with people in all parts of the school district in order to stay in touch with their needs and concerns. This practice was first used at Hewlett-Packard and has been used in a variety of forms in many of the best-run companies. Management by wandering around is not easy; it is an art that requires the execution of four critical steps.

Connecting. The first step in managing by wandering around is to connect with people—get out into the schools and meet them. The managers of the best-run companies have thought of a number of ways to show that they are committed to connecting with their stakeholders. For example:

- Sam Walton of Wal-Mart stores visits each of over seven hundred stores annually to connect with his people.

- Phil Staley, who has turned around an old Ford plant in Edison, New Jersey, hosts a steak barbecue as part of his effort to connect with the people at Ford.

- Jimmy Treybig, founder of Tandem Computer, holds a "beer bust" once a week to connect with his people.

- Chairman Roger Milliken of Milliken Company can be seen lecturing at the Milliken Customer Service Center in Spartanburg, South Carolina, to connect with customers.

- Hewlett-Packard engineers leave their individual project out on the bench so that other engineers can connect with what they are working on. As a result, everybody has an opportunity to get into the act.

- Jock Zenger, president of the Syntex Corporation, eats breakfast at the same table in the company cafeteria about two times weekly to stay in touch with his people.

I believe that the best way to connect with people on a consistent basis is to set aside certain days and times to wander around. In this way, this practice will become a routine part of your schedule and not something that is incidental to it.

Once you have made contact with a person or a small group, explain why you are there—for example "to keep in touch with our most important asset." The point of the meeting is to hear *their* concerns, to learn what *they* think about their jobs and the school district. It might help to start off the meeting with a leading question, such as, "What are some of the most pressing problems in this school district?" "What do you like least about this school district?" "What should I do that I am not doing?" "Are you satisfied with how we treat you?"

Listening. After you have connected with people in the school district and have begun the meeting with some questions, the second and most crucial step in the process is listening. Listening means taking an interest in what is being said without judging or evaluating; it calls for openness and objectivity. Listening is a form of caring. No administrator can be caring and concerned about people unless he or she knows them as human beings. No administrator can know his or her people unless they disclose, reveal, and unveil themselves. And no administrator can initiate meaningful dialogue with people unless he or she seriously listens. Genuine listening is a very difficult task. It takes conscious effort and hard work to become an effective listener. Whenever an administrator is preoccupied or concerned solely with himself or herself, receptivity is at a low level. Unless a conscious effort is made to get in tune with an individual, real listening cannot occur.

There are several keys to successful listening:

- Stop talking. A person cannot listen if he or she is busy talking or thinking about what to say next.
- Be attentive. Some administrators seem to be listening, but they are thinking about something else and thus are not connected to the other person who is talking. A true listener is one who is quiet and sensitive to what is being said in an active, open, receptive, and genuine manner. A true listener is one who is inwardly silent. A true listener does not immediately evaluate or judge what is being said, but acts as a receptacle for verbal and nonverbal messages.

- Be patient. People need time to reveal themselves at their own pace and in their own manner. If an administrator tries to force the listening process, the connection with the speaker will collapse.
- Obtain clarity. At times the creative listener will respond, reflect, express understanding, or request clarity. During this process, which Carl Rogers calls reflective listening, the administrator may request more information or may paraphrase what

is being said in order to determine what the speaker is really thinking and thus facilitate communication.

- Show empathy. School people will open up to an administrator more freely if they feel that he or she shares or is sensitive to their thoughts and feelings.

- Be attentive on two levels. People tend to converse on two levels. The first level is the superficial one. On this level, people will often voice concerns, interests, desires, and aspirations that are petty or that have nothing to do with their true thoughts or feelings. It is as if they needed a springboard to propel them into the next level. This is the level at which the real intent of the conversation and the person's real goals are expressed. The only way to detect which level a person is communicating on is to let him or her continue talking. Sooner or later, you will learn of the real intent of the conversation. A listener needs a great deal of skill to decipher when a person has moved to the second level in the conversation. If an administrator does not allow the person to move from the superficial level to the second level because of impatience, lack of time, or preoccupation, the real intent of the conversation may never be revealed.

- Observe nonverbal communication. People tend to express almost twice as much nonverbally as they do with words. Therefore, one effective listening technique is for the administrator to to read the nonverbal actions of a speaker. A greater understanding of how we all communicate nonverbally will also help the administrator to improve his or

169

her own body language, and eliminate body language that transmits negative cues.

- Avoid arguing or interruptive behavior. Some administrators have a tendency to get overly involved or to react emotionally to what is being said. This will do nothing but stifle the communication process. The effective listener will avoid falling into this trap by not jumping to conclusions.

Facilitating. There are several reasons an administrator should manage by wandering around. One of these is to become aware of the concerns of school district employees. During conversations with people throughout the district, the administrator will occasionally learn of concerns or situations that if left unaddressed could develop into full-scale problems. When this kind of concern is expressed, the administrator must move into the third phase in the process of management by wandering around facilitating. Facilitating involves two skills: (1) asking probing questions that will help a speaker convey his thoughts, attitudes, and feelings accurately and completely and (2) paraphrasing the speaker's words so as to ensure that the administrator has interpreted those words correctly.

Follow-through. The fourth step in management by wandering around is a very deliberate one that must be executed with a great deal of sensitivity. Upon arriving back at the office, the administrator asks to review the notes of his or her meetings and conversations and look for similarities in the concerns people have expressed. Once a problem has been identified, the next step is to take action either directly or by delegating authority. If the problem that is identified lies in the domain of one particular supervisor, the appropriate course is to inform him or her of the concern and its intensity, (without ever divulging sources) discuss possible courses of action, and request that he or she address the concern within five days and submit a written report on the solution. Meanwhile the administrator should report to the persons involved, indicating steps that are being taken to resolve the concern. A word of caution: When discussing the concern with the administrator involved, be very cordial, avoid arguing, and use the discussion as an opportunity to explore alternative solutions to the problem and what can be done to prevent the situation from reappearing. After a common understanding has been arrived at, thank the person for his or her time. Later, a note of thanks for his or her cooperative efforts should be sent to the administrator.

How the Best Wander

The best-run companies tend to use creative ways to stay in touch with the stakeholders—employees, vendors, and customers. Following are some ways in which the managers of these companies wander around, connecting, listening, facilitating, and following through with people.

- Domino's Pizza Distribution Company regularly conducts Vendor Appreciation Days. On these occasion scores of Domino's people converge on a Wisconsin cheesemaker, for example, or a California olive grower, to thank these vendors for the manner in which they have served them. Domino's

171

includes in its philosophy a statement identifying vendors as a part of its family.

- Frank Perdue goes around his plants giving impromptu talks to groups of his people concerning product quality.

- Hewlett-Packard conducts "focus meetings" in which customers are assembled in groups to discuss products.

How to Implement Management by Wandering Around

There is no set procedure for implementing management by wandering around. However, I believe that the following steps should enable any school district to implement the practice with a high degree of success.

- Endorse the practice of management by wandering around in the district's statement of philosophy.

- Bring in a consultant to train central and building administrators in listening and facilitating skills. Make certain that the training involves everyone in role playing.

- Help school people to identify who the stakeholders of the school district are, and emphasize the need to stay in touch with them in order to achieve excellence. Indicate what activities should be engaged in to stay in touch with the stakeholders.

- Prepare administrative guidelines that suggest the

minimum time each administrator should devote to managing by wandering around.

- Take into consideration the degree to which administrators manage by wandering around when evaluating their performance.

- Make certain all school people are informed of the administrators' schedule for wandering around.

Strategies for Achieving Excellence

- Have each central administrator spend one full day with kids, discovering what they like and dislike about school. In addition, require each member of the central administration team to spend an entire week in a school interviewing parents, helping teachers, and assisting custodians and maintenance people. Then arrange for the entire central administration team to go on a retreat and discuss the various perceptions they have encountered in their schools, as well as ways in which improvements can be made in these perceptions by changing the way the school district operates. Report conclusions to all stakeholders, and keep them informed of progress in making improvements.

- Arrange to meet with a different group of parents or other stakeholders each quarter to ask them "How are we doing for your kids?" Take notes, discuss alternative solutions to problems, and indicate when the parents or other stakeholders can look for changes.

- Invite book vendors, students, and teachers to a

meeting where both students and teachers can critique texts, kits, and other materials.

- Bring in parents who send their kids to private schools and ask them why they chose not to use the public schools. When appropriate and feasible, make changes based on their comments.

- Supplement the management by wandering around process in the following ways:

  — Install a toll-free phone number that kids and parents can use to express their concerns. Require central administrators to listen in on the calls whenever possible.

  — In each building, in a location everybody will see it, place a special bulletin board for displaying letters. Post complimentary letters on the right side and uncomplimentary letters on the left side. Indicate in the school district's newsletter the steps that are being taken to address concerns reported in the uncomplimentary letters.

  — Each month give a reward to the student who submits the best idea for improving the school. Do the same for a parent.

Establish a Succession Program

Succession planning has suddenly emerged as a prime managerial concern.
—Management Review

Although many of the best-run companies such as IBM, Procter & Gamble, Delta Air Lines, Exxon, Hewlett Packard, and 3M have succession plans, there is very little information available about how the plans are constructed. Harry Levinson and Stuart Rosenthal, co-authors of *CEO*, indicate in their book that the CEOs of many successful companies—people such as Reginald H. Tore of G.E., Walter B. Wriston of Citicorp, Ian K. MacGregor of AMAX, John W. Hanley of Monsanto Company, and Thomas J. Watson of IBM—are preoccupied with who will succeed them as CEO. In the words of the authors, "Each has a dominating concern for the future of his organization." Exxon's succession program began as early as 1929, when President Walter Teagle laid down the law that every manager had to identify and train a successor. Today, all managers at Exxon are required to develop a systematic succession plan for their own position and for every position they supervise.

I have done some research on the topic of succession programs and have designed a succession plan that I believe accommodates the needs of school districts. I call this the Four-Tier Comprehensive Succession Program.

The Four-Tier Comprehensive Succession Program is a systematic process for educating, training, and developing selected school people to assume administrative and supervisory positions as steps in a controlled career-path program. Each person is carefully selected, and then his or her strengths are identified and improved on and weaknesses eliminated through a variety of educational, training, and development activities that take place over a period of years.

The succession program contains four graduated tiers. Tier 1 is designed to develop assistant principals. Tier 2 is set up to groom elementary, junior high, and secondary school principals. Tier 3 is designed to prepare central administrators and supervisors. And Tier 4 is established to prepare superintendents of schools. The succession program dovetails with the performance evaluation program and the development program that should already exist in the district. The growth and development of each person in a tier is carefully observed and monitored. The succession program is designed to accommodate changing conditions within and outside the district.

The Four-Tier Succession Program is based on the following assumptions:

- Promotion from within is an important value of the school organization and is strictly enforced.

- The school district is committed to "growing its own."

- Training and development are an important component of the total school system.

176

- Politics do not play any part in the succession program.

In addition to the philosophical assumptions mentioned above, the following assumptions should guide the way in which the succession program is managed.

- The department of human resources, or personnel department is responsible for managing the entire succession program.

- All records of persons participating in the succession program are updated in a timely manner.

- Promotions are made based on the assessment of each team and the recommendation of the superintendent, and are subject to the approval of the school board. Enrollment in the succession program does not guarantee that one will be promoted to any position.

- In order for a person to be eligible for a certain position, he or she must successfully have completed all the requirements associated with the tier that encompasses the position.

There are several reasons for developing a succession program:

- To ensure organizational continuity in the event that a position becomes vacant, or one reason or another.

- To improve morale by demonstrating to school people that they have an opportunity to attain any position in the school district provided they meet certain requirements.

- To provide a formal program that integrates training, development, and education with career development and performance evaluation review.

- To actualize the policy of promotion from within by ensuring that the school district has a group of well trained people from which it can select to fill various administrative and supervisory positions.

There are six steps in the execution of the Four-Tier Comprehensive Succession Program.

The first step is for the human resources department to describe all of the various activities that will be needed to educate, develop, and train the school people enrolled in the succession program. These activities are the heart of the Four-Tier Comprehensive Succession Program. Each of the following activities will enable the nominee to improve one or more skills:

Participating in professional organizations. Those enrolled in the succession program not only are required to become members of three professional organizations directly related to their specific tier, but are also required to attend annual conferences of at least two of the organizations and to describe in writing what they have learned by becoming a member of the organizations and by attending the annual conferences. In addition, each person is required to demonstrate how his or her membership in these organizations and activities has improved his or her effectiveness. Each person in Tiers 3 and 4 is required to become a member of an organization not directly related to education and to attend its annual conference. An example of appropriate organizations would be the American Management Association, and the National Association of Quality Circles.

Reading. Each person within each tier is required to

read certain classic texts on school administration and supervision as well as specific books. The person must write up a critical analysis of each book and give at least three concrete examples of how the book has helped him or her have a positive impact on people he or she serves.

Thus a person who progresses from Tier 1 to Tier 4 would have read and digested a minimum of 50 books on school administration and supervision. Each person's critical analyses are included in his or her permanent record.

Exercising Communication Skills. Although each person enrolled in the succession program must already have demonstrated satisfactory skills in speaking and writing, communication skills can always be strengthened, and to this end each person will be required to engage in certain activities.

All those participating in Tier 1 are required to prepare several reports and presentations to be delivered to school people and community groups. All participants in Tier 2 are required to prepare a minimum of five written projects involving either research, proposal writing, or an evaluation of a program. In addition, all individuals in this tier are required to conduct a minimum of three 30-minute presentations before a group of their peers. Each person in Tier 3 is required to prepare a manual describing a step-by-step process for performing a managerial or supervisory task, such as facilitating consensus decision making or conducting a post-observation conference. In addition, each person is required to prepare a written proposal for funding and submit it to an organization. The proposal must be deemed acceptable by the superintendent prior to submission. All participants in Tier 4 are required to give a minimum of three workshops or lectures at the annual conference of the organization of which they are members.

Demonstrating Expertise. Each person enrolled in Tiers 3 and 4 is required to demonstrate expertise in at least one area relevant to the tier in which he or she is enrolled. For example, for Tier 3 an appropriate area of expertise would be mastery learning. For Tier 4, strategic thinking and planning would be appropriate areas. It is not sufficient merely to acquire training in a field; there must be some evidence that the person is recognized as an expert in this area—for example, the publication of several scholarly articles or a book.

Rotating Jobs. Job rotation is recommended for people in Tiers 3 and 4. A person enrolled in Tier 3 of the program might be required to rotate through at least five different positions and spend at least one full year in each. For example, an enrollee might be required to be assume responsibilities in areas such as language arts, math, special education, personnel, guidance, testing, or adult education. Enrollees in Tier 4 should be required to acquire at least one year or a minimum total of five years of experience through job placement in the areas of human resources (personnel), administration, research and development, business administration, and curriculum and instruction.

Carrying Out Project Assignments and Special Assignments. At times individuals may be assigned to perform a particular function in a project. For example, a Tier 1 person might be invited to volunteer to become a member of a circle of excellence, a Tier 2 person could be asked to serve as a leader of a circle of excellence, or a Tier 3 person could be asked to serve as a facilitator of the circle of excellence program. Enrollees might also be required to participate in other special assignments. For example, if the superintendent saw the need to organize a team to study the problem of low teacher morale, a Tier 3 or 4 person might be assigned to head the team, and Tier 1 and 2 persons might be assigned to become members. Project assignments and special assignments should be an expected part of training and development activities for every person in each tier.

Attending Special Training. Those enrolled at the Tier 4 level might be assigned additional training and development activities depending on conditions. For example, if the superintendent saw a need to train all Tier 4 people in strategic planning, each person may be required to attend a course at The Planning Executives Institute at 5500 College Corner Pike, Oxford, Ohio. Or, if the superintendent was interested in fostering intrapreneurship throughout the school district, Tier 4 persons might be required to attend appropriate courses of the International Institute of Intrapreneurs at Cedar Swamp Rd., Deep River, Connecticut.

Visiting Other Schools. To ensure that they stay abreast of what other school districts are doing, all enrollees are required to visit schools that have implemented practices and programs worthy of emulation. In Tier 1, all participants are required to visit a minimum of five local school districts to observe and discuss matters pertinent to their particular tier. In Tier 2, all participants are required to visit six school districts of which three should be local and the remaining three should be located elsewhere in the country. In Tiers 3 and 4, all enrollees should visit six school districts nation-wide that have exemplary programs and practices. Each visitation must be followed by a written report and recommendations to the superintendent as to what principles, programs, or practices should be emulated by the school district.

The second essential step in developing the succession program is for the human resources department to develop a strand of competencies that each enrollee must master in order to be promoted to a different position or to move between tiers in the succession program. All of the current and future duties for positions represented by each tier should be identified, After all of the duties have been identified, the type of behavior and/or attitudes expected of the enrollee as a result of one or more learning activities should be described. There are three types of competency, all of which should be considered:

- Knowledge competency deals exclusively with the cognitive domain—that is, it pertains only to mental activities. Knowledge competency can be demonstrated directly through verbal and/or written responses.

- Skill competency involves the cognitive domain as well as the psychomotor domain—both mental and physical activities. Skill competency can be demonstrated directly through physical and mental performance.

- Attitudinal competency involves the affective domain. It may pertain to the values, attitudes, and interests acquired from cognitive and/or a psychomotor activity. Attitudinal competency is an indirect competency; because it is intangible. It can be evaluated only in terms of associated behaviors that can be explained in specific and observable terms. Attitudinal competency can be demonstrated through written responses and/or performances.

A specific tier and its accompanying competencies might be described as follows:

Tier 1 Position:
Assistant Principal

Current Duty	Competencies
To demonstrate a systematic humanistic teacher evaluation	Enrollee is able to perform a teacher evaluation that satisfies the criteria listed below. A team of peers will evaluate the enrollee and will determine that the teacher evaluation has been conducted satisfactorily if there has been an 80% improvement in the skills since the last assessment.

- The performance review is conducted in a systematic manner as prescribed by policy.
- The post-observation conference is opened in a firm but friendly manner.
- Sufficient time is allocated for the observation and the post-observation conference.
- The evaluator is supportive.
- Problems are anticipated and expected.

183

- Some disagreement is anticipated and allowed.
- A win-win climate is evident.
- Steps for improving the performance are mutually agreed upon.
- A subsequent date and time for reviewing the performance are agreed upon.

Future duty
To train teachers to implement peer and reverse-performance reviews.

The enrollee is able to train teachers to conduct peer reviews and reviews of their immediate supervisors as well as of support staff. This competency is deemed satisfactorily achieved when the teachers who have been trained to conduct peer reviews are favorably evaluated on the basis of the criteria described above. An additional indication that teachers have been successfully trained is consensus among those being reviewed that the recommendations that were given resulted in improved performance.

The third step is to organize a succession committee. This committee should have the assistant superintendent for human resources as the leader, and an outstanding psychologist, principal, supervisor, and teacher as members. The job of this committee is to select participants for the program.

Once the succession committee has been established, it can invite school administrators to nominate people directly under their supervision for the succession program. Administrators identify individuals who are in their judgment currently or potentially qualified for a school administration or supervision position. They then draw up a statement justifying their assessment of the person they have nominated, including in the statement a description of the nominee's strengths, as well as his or her experiences, such as participation in a task force.

Their are certain minimum educational requirements for nomination to the succession program, including not only certain degrees and course work, but also specific state certifications. A minimum requirement for acceptance in any tier of the succession program is the Master's degree. For Tier 1, temporary certification as a building principal is also needed. For Tier 2, 30 college credits are required, as well as permanent state certification as a building principal. To enter the succession program on Tier 3, a nominee must have a professional diploma and permanent state certification as a district administrator. A Tier 4 nominee must have a Ph.D. or Ed.D. degree in educational administration and permanent state certification as a district administrator.

It is then the responsibility of the district's human resources department to test nominees and compile information on each of them, including:

- Personal history record
- Self-analysis
- Results of written and oral English tests
- Results of personality test
- Results of interest test
- Results of performance review
- Reference checks
- Results of managerial-skills test
- Academic record
- Results of peer evaluations

After the nominations have been submitted, various tests have been administered to the nominees and results obtained, and other subjective and objective information has been compiled, it is the succession committee's job to read and evaluate the information on each nominee. When the committee is satisfied that it has critically scrutinized all of the compiled information and discussed the merits of each nomination, each nominee is invited to appear before the committee for an interview. After each interview, another discussion is conducted regarding the nominee. Finally a decision is reached by the committee either to accept or reject the nomination. Whenever the committee rejects a nominee, a letter should be sent to that person and to the nominator stating the reason for the rejection. A list of all those who have been accepted should be shared with all administrators and supervisors as well as with the school board.

The next step for the committee is to assign a mentor

to each person accepted for participation in the succession program. Usually the mentor will be the immediate supervisor of the enrollee; however if this is not feasible for some reason, another supervisor may be assigned as a mentor to an enrollee.

The fourth step is to prepare a Five-Year Development Plan for each enrollee. This step should be performed jointly by the succession committee, the mentor, and the enrollee. All parties convene at a meeting to agree on the strengths, weaknesses, needs and placement of the enrollee, using all of the information compiled in Step 3. Based on this information, the personal aspirations of the enrollee, and the activities described in Step 1, the group prepares for each enrollee a Five-Year Development Plan, which is then updated yearly through the Individual Development Plan.

Following are the essential components of the Five-Year Development Plan:

- Strengths. Give examples of the enrollee's strengths as observed from the current position.

- Weaknesses. Indicate examples of weaknesses, as observed from the enrollee's present position.

- Aspiration/Goals. Describe the interests and aspirations expressed by the enrollee.

- Estimated Potential. Give the highest position the enrollee is currently expected to attain.

- Five-Year Assignment. Indicate recommended assignments for the enrollee over the next five years.

- Five-Year Self-Development Actions. Indicate all activities the enrollee is presently taking or planning to take to supplement his or her various assignments.

- Year-by-Year Assignment. Indicate the substance of the annual progress review, highlighting what progress has been made, what areas need improvements and what steps should be taken to improve performance growth. In addition, recommended additional training and development activities for the ensuing school year.

The fifth step is to prepare the Annual Development Plan. The enrollee uses the Five-Year Development Plan (and the last Annual Development Plan in years after the first) to develop an Annual Development Plan. This step is carried out annually. The plan must be approved either by the assistant superintendent for human resources or by the enrollee's supervisor, and is the basis by which he or she continues in the succession program.

Following are the essential components of the Annual Development Plan:

- Competencies to Be Mastered. Indicate here all of the competencies that the enrollee intends to master during the school year in question. These competencies should come directly from the list for the enrollee's particular tier, and should be agreed upon by both the nominee and the succession committee.

- Assignment Plan. Describe the types of responsibilities, work assignments, and projects the enrollee will engage in to further develop his or her potential. The description should include the location of the assignment, the supervisor, duration, and dates of placement and termination.

- Training and Education Plan. Include all of the coaching, training, and educational activities that the enrollee will engage in to supplement his or her assignment.

Step 6 is assessment. Key elements in the Four-Tier Comprehensive Succession Program are the quarterly and annual reviews that take place to track each enrollee's progress. These are intended to substitute for the traditional performance review; to highlight strengths, weaknesses, and areas needing improvement; to cite those activities that will enable the enrollee to stay abreast of changing conditions; and to prescribe for each individual a comprehensive course of training, development, and education that will complement the school district's efforts to "grow its own" competent administrators and supervisors. The assessment should be conducted as follows:

- Every ten weeks of the school year an assessment should be conducted to determine the degree to which the assessments enabled the enrollee to master the competencies; assess all of the training and education activities undertaken by the enrollees to master the competencies; determine how progress was measured and what degree of progress was made; and validate the satisfactory assignment of each competency with a signature from a supervisor or evaluator.

- The annual review should be an overall assessment of the enrollee's progress based on all previous assessments, and should indicate whether the enrollee is progressing up to his or her potential. The annual review should include recommendations of ways to improve those areas that need improvement. These recommendations should be considered first when the Individual Development Plan for the next school year is prepared.

Strategies for Achieving Excellence

- Contact the American Association of School Administrators and state departments of education to find out if they have information on school districts that have established a succession program. If so, make arrangements to visit these school districts. If not, contact the companies indicated in this lesson and request an appointment to visit them to discuss their succession program.

- Attend the American Management Association's next workshop on succession planning.

- Look in the library for books and journals that contain articles on succession planning, such as the *Training and Development Journal*, published by the American Society for Training and Development, and study them.

- Submit a proposal you develop for a succession program to at least three management development and succession-planning consultants. Contact the American Society for Training and Development located in Madison, Wisconsin, for a list of these consultants. The consultants should assess how well the proposal covers the following important areas:

  — The integration of performance evaluation and training and development

— Strategic planning for long-term human-resource needs
— Accomodation of changing times and conditions
— Five- to ten-year span
— Nomination and selection process
— Periodic and annual reviews
— Lateral and vertical movements
— Types of forms required
— Techniques for monitoring growth and progress
— How job assignments are made
— Types of committees needed to establish and maintain the program
— How the program is conducted across school district, school, and team lines.

• Lesson 13 •

Address the Whole Person

Society in recent years has assimilated repeated
reminders of the first principle of ecology: that
everything affects every-thing else, mind, body,
spirit; work, home, play; individual organization,
society; earth, air, water, energy, economy.
—W. Mathew Tuechter and Tom Utne

As we have seen, best-run companies show a gener-
alized concern for the welfare of their people as a natural
part of the working relationship. Many of these companies have moved beyond simply satisfying employees'
economic needs and have become equally concerned
about their physiological and psychological needs. To
address these concerns, some companies have established what have become known as "wellness programs,"—that is, programs created to keep the company's human resources in good physical and mental
health. A wellness program is made up of a variety of
activities designed to maintain and improve the physical
and psychological fitness of employees. A complete wellness program includes the following:

• A complete medical examination as a means to
establish baseline data.

- Nutritious meals during lunch and special events.

- Monitoring of progress.

- Employee advisory resources.

- Facilities for various sports or physical fitness activities such as jogging, Nautilus workouts, etc.

We can no longer ignore the fact that thousands of our teachers are affected by alcoholism and a growing number are beginning to use narcotics, or the fact that too many of our teachers and administrators are still smoking even though they are aware of the risk of getting cancer. We can no longer look the other way as stress takes its toll on thousands upon thousands of our teachers and other school people, and we can no longer ignore the excess weight and the poor health of many of our teachers and administrators. We have the ways and means to address the whole person, and we can take cues from what the best-run companies are doing to keep their people in good physical and mental health.

What the Best Are Doing?

Nissan Corporation encourages employees to participate in calisthenics or other physical activities on a daily basis and has set up pingpong tables and basketball hoops throughout the company's 75-acre plant. In addition baseball diamonds and volleyball courts are located outside the plant. Employees make good use of these facilities during lunch and morning and afternoon breaks. Nissan recently constructed an activity center which includes Nautilus weight-training equipment, a full-sized swimming pool, and saunas.

Baxter Travenol Laboratories has installed in a section of its headquarters a gymnasium a place where people can work out and attend health and fitness classes. Over 900 employees—more than 50 percent of Baxter's people—pay an annual fee of $50 to participate in the varied wellness activities at Baxter. In 1983 the company installed an outdoor half-mile jogging track.

Perhaps the most effective wellness program is the one established by Hospital Corporation of America, where employees get paid for keeping themselves physically fit. In 1979 HCA initiated what is referred to as "Aerobic Challenge." To qualify for this program, all HCA people must meet certain minimum requirements, such as running 30 miles or playing at least 15 hours of racquet ball. Once a person has qualified for the program, he or she is reimbursed for exercising at a set rate per mile (for swimming or running, for example) or per hour (racquetball or other sports). Some of the rates are as follows:

- Swimming: 96 cents per mile
- Running/Walking: 24 cents per mile
- Bicycling: 6 cents per mile
- Aerobic Dancing/Jazzercise: 96 cents per hour
- Racquet Ball: 48 cents per hour

Nearly 50 percent of the 900 people at HCA are in the plan. The average participant in 1982 received $146; one employee earned $800.

Levi Strauss has installed a soundproof room, where employees can retire after a hard day to get rid of their pent-up emotions by banging on the walls or chanting mantras.

Johnson & Johnson also has an excellent employee health plan. The program is called "Live for Life." A large fitness center is made available for employees who desire to work out. However, the program is more comprehensive in scope. All participants must undergo a physical examination, which is used by professionals to guide each person in a physical fitness program geared to his or her individual needs. The program also stresses eating the proper foods and eliminating addictive habits such as smoking and drinking.

At Tenneco, Inc. the top two floors of the Ten-Ten Garage are designated as the Tenneco Employee Center. The top floor contains an employee cafeteria, various meeting rooms, and an indoor patio garden with live trees to create an outdoor feeling. On the next floor is a $11 million health and fitness center that contains four racquetball courts, exercise rooms with Nautilus equipment, an all-purpose athletic room, saunas, jacuzzi, pool, and a one-fifth-mile track. The center is operated by a health and fitness manager and with a staff of 11 people. Some 600 Tenneco people use the center each day, more than 1800 employees regularly visit the center. The center provides all of the clothing needed for the various activities. Before using the fitness center, employees must submit to a complete medical examination. A computer with five terminals is used to track the individual progress of each participant.

Control Data Corporation has one of the most comprehensive wellness programs in the country. The company's Stay Well Program includes:

- Attractive promotional booklets entitled "Join the Stay Well Program and Feel Like a Million."

- A health news magazine for employees and their families entitled *Well Times*, which features summaries of articles from medical journals and newspapers and reports of studies from research centers to help keep employees and their families informed of developments that affect their health.

- Health assessment to identify an employee's health history and those aspects of his or her current life styles that affect health. The health assessment includes interpretation sessions during which each participant's health assessment is explained and specific recommendations are made as to what lifestyle changes would improve the participant's health.

- Education programs designed to teach individuals more about their health and life styles. These courses are offered in three variations:

  — Computer-based courses. Based on an individual's responses, the computer will coach the person on lifestyle changes that would improve his or her health.

  — Self-study course. Some courses are similar to correspondence courses in that they are designed to be convenient for the participant.

  — Group courses for those who enjoy attending class with friends and peers, other classes are led by professional instructors.

- Action teams, which are intended to encourage participants to join together as teams to give each other moral support in meeting wellness goals.

- An employee advisory resource service to assist employees and their families in solving personal work-related problems through 24-hour phone counseling, referral, and face-to-face counseling.

What Can a School District Do?

What steps should a school district take to institute a successful physical and psychological fitness program? There are several:

- Obtain central administration support. Obviously, no wellness program can reach its full potential unless central administrators provide visible support. The ideal support would include the superintendent's religiously participating in all of the activities, thereby serving as a role model. T. Boone Pickens, CEO of Mesa Petroleum, engages in a daily workout program in the company's gym. In addition, he reinforces the importance of staying well and fit whenever he is interviewing new or potential employees.

- Promote the program with the school board. The school district will have to provide a budget to initiate the program and may have to continue this support throughout the life of the program. During difficult times, some board members may be inclined to eliminate the program by not supporting it with an adequate budget. It is up to the administrator to convince them that, if the school district is serious about treating its employees as its greatest asset, it will not tamper with this program.

- Provide for School People Ownership. When people are actively involved in all aspects of a program, they are more inclined to support it. There are several ways to establish a sense of ownership of the health and fitness program among school people. One way is to establish a health-conscious school environment by fostering a support culture that includes peers, leaders among teachers and administrators, members of employees' families, and retirees. Another way to promote a sense of ownership of the program is to organize an Employee Wellness Council which develops policies and procedures, maintains communication among school people, provides leadership, and participates in the planning and organizing of appropriate health and fitness events. Finally, the district might emulate those companies that have found that requiring a small program fee creates a sense of ownership and value among the participants. Add incentive for participants. Added incentive for participants to remain active with the program can be created by having the district match the amount of money collected through membership dues.

- Maintain professional leadership. Experience has indicated that the most successful programs are those that are led by dynamic leaders—people who obviously care for and are concerned about the health and welfare of the employees. Those companies that have established wellness programs have designated someone to oversee the program on a continuous basis. It is desirable for the leaders not only to be trained in physical and health education, but also to have outstanding motivational skills, and high enthusiasm for the program and a fun-loving attitude.

- Plan the program carefully. When planning is initiated, it will become evident that much space and equipment are necessary for a truly comprehensive program of strength, endurance, and physical activities. Ordinarily, school districts allocate funds for physical education and locker facilities; however, many schools do not have adequate space for health classes, counseling, Nautilus and weight-training equipment, and other equipment that is part of a good wellness program. Keep in mind that although equipment is important to provide an adequate and comprehensive program, the emphasis should always be on school people. If you begin using the equipment and resources that are already available in the district and concentrate on instilling a concern for good health among employees, the wellness program will get off to a good start.

- Gather baseline data. Prior to the implementation of the wellness program, it is imperative that adequate baseline data be compiled on such variables as health-care costs, absenteeism, fitness levels, employee morale, and employee health risks. This information will be used as a basis for evaluating the effectiveness of the program and providing justification for continued funding of the program.

- Make provisions to educate school people on the need for physical and psychological fitness. Both employees and students should be involved in promoting the program. The essential element in producing an effective wellness program is to establish a "health culture" throughout the school environment. To this end special efforts must be made to "get to" those school people who are not otherwise likely to respond, through a variety of outreach activities such as nutritional programs in the cafeteria, health newsletters, poster campaigns, special events, and various other activities developed around a health and mental fitness theme. An especially good motivator is to have noted health experts visit the school district to conduct health and mental fitness discussions with both the students and the employees. (Because this aspect of the program may be more than the program can pay for through membership fees and the school district's reimbursement policy, I suggest that an allocation for this expense be included in the general budget.) Other methods of improving motivation and awareness of physical and mental fitness include goal setting, reinforcement through games and contests, and establishing various incentives such as pins, award certificates, T-shirts, and individual recognition. Art classes can design brochures, and English and Health classes can prepare creative booklets and pamphlets to create an awareness of positive health habits.

- Make certain that the program requires each participant to be assessed by a health professional. Such assessment will minimize the risk of a person's engaging in unsuitable or overly strenuous exercise, as well as allow each participant to establish a personalized program that meets his or her individual needs. The school physician, the physical education, health education, and home economics teachers are professionals who might be offered special compensation to conduct such health assessments. At times it may be necessary to refer to participants outside the school to community resources and health professionals for initial assessments.

I believe it would be fitting for me to mention briefly a program that could serve as a model for other school districts. The DeKalb County School District of Decatur, Georgia, has established one of the finest human resources departments in the nation under the guidance of Dean Grant, Director of Personnel for Staff Services. Dean Grant is always seeking new ways to improve services for the school district's 4000 people. One of his recent innovations is a computerized life assessment program. This program evaluates a person's life experiences, medical history, and leisure time, and then comes up with a prescription for extending his or her life. Armed with the computerized prescription, health professionals confer with each school person to explain how he or she could live a more healthy and extended life. The school district started this program with its administrators and then offered it to all employees. The school district's rationale for establishing the life assessment program is that healthier employees are happier and perform better.

Establishing a wellness program is a way to enhance the quality of life and morale of school people as well as to make them more productive. There is no doubt that in the future more and more organizations will begin to address the whole person and provide concerned and assertive leadership in an effort to gain the "fitness edge" with healthier and happier people.

Strategies for Achieving Excellence

- Do what Control Data has done—publish a quarterly health news magazine for employees and their families. You may wish to use Control Data Corporation's *Well Times* as a a model. Copies can be obtained from the Managing Editor, Well Times, c/o Control Data Corporation, P.O. Box O, HQS 1/S, Minneapolis, MN 55440.

- Establish a 24-hour-a-day telephone hotline so that school people with physical or mental health problems have quick and easy access to assistance whenever they need it, and an opportunity to call anonymously.

- Contact the companies mentioned in this lesson and request that they forward to you materials on their employee wellness programs. Use these materials as models to help produce policies, guidelines, newsletters, and other materials for your own program.

- Establish wellness teams made up of friends, co-workers, and spouses who meet to give each other moral support as they participate in a wellness program and begin to change their life styles. Wellness teams can get together for such fitness or exercise activities as jogging, walking, or aerobic dance.

- Seek professional assistance firms or individuals with experience in establishing wellness programs.

One such firm is Control Data Corporation. In 1976, Control Data and its subsidiary, Commercial Credit, began marketing their knowledge and experience in organizing and operating employee assistance programs. Since then, the corporation has assisted more than 150 small businesses to establish their own programs. Some organizations request short-term consultation to evaluate and improve existing programs. Others request more comprehensive consultation, which can include reviewing employee relations policies and procedures, conducting management training in employee assistance, or orienting employees to the program. For further information contact Employee Advisory Resource, Control Data, P.O. Box O, Minneapolis, MN 55440. Another resource person who could assist you in establishing your own wellness program is Richard O. Keeblor, President and CEO of Living Well in America, based in Houston, Texas.

Contact the President's Council for Physical Fitness and Sports in Atlanta, Georgia, to obtain information on employee health and fitness programs and on the symposium offered by the Council.

- Contact the Hospital Corporation of America in Nashville, Tennessee, or the Bonnie Bell Cosmetic Corporation, Lakeland, Ohio, to get information on how these companies provide financial incentives for employees who meet certain wellness requirements. Consider including this practice in your wellness program.

- Contact the Washington Business Group on Health and the Association for Fitness in Business in

Washington, D.C., for a list of companies with outstanding wellness programs, and visit at least three of these companies.

- Persuade local physicians or mental health professionals to participate in the district's Wellness Council.

- Visit Tenneco in Houston to observe its program in action.

Notes

Introduction: It Takes Visionary People to Achieve Excellence

I gathered my thoughts for portions of this lesson from Gifford Pinchot III's *Intrapreneuring* (New York: Harper & Row, 1985), pp. 126-136 and pp. 154-159; from Thomas A. Peters and Nancy Austin's *A Passion for Excellence* (New York: Random House, 1985), p. 4, reprinted by permission, and from Craig R. Hickman & Michael A. Silva's *Creating Excellence* (New York: New American Library, 1984), pp. 149-173.

Lesson 1: Attain Excellence Through Ownership

An excellent book on the three human addictions is Kenneth Keyes, Jr.'s *Handbook to Higher Consciousness* (Marina del Rey Calif.: DeVorss, 1972). Another excellent book that will give you some insight into personal goal fulfillment is Charles L. Hughes's *Goal-Setting: Key to Individual and Organizational Effectiveness* (New York: American Management Association, 1965). Thomas Peters and Nancy Austin's *A Passion for Excellence* (New York: Random House,1985) pp. 213-251, was of invaluable assistance to me.

Lesson 2: Achieve a Balance Between Loose and Tight Policies

The essence of this lesson came primarily from my own personal experience and from Thomas Peters and

Robert Waterman's *In Search of Excellence* (New York: Harper & Row, 1982), pp. 318-325.

Lesson 3: Become More Egalitarian

Not much has been written about egalitarianism. I was fortunate to come across a book by Evan Luard, *Socialism Without the State* (New York: St. Martin's Press, 1979), which aided me tremendously in writing this lesson.

Lesson 4: Use a Personal Computer at the Top

Much of the substance of this lesson came from an article entitled "Personal Computer at the Top" that appeared in the March 1985 issue of *Personal Computer*, pp. 68-79. Used with permission.

Lesson 5: Become Research and Development Oriented

Two valuable sources were Rosabeth Moss Kanter's *The Change Masters* (New York: Simon & Schuster, 1983), p. 19, and Peter F. Drucker's *Innovation and Entrepreneurship* (New York: Harper & Row, 1985), pp. 35, 134-138, 186. I also made good use of the printed materials that were shared with me by some of the best-run companies.

Lesson 6: Revamp the Process of Selecting Teachers

Descriptions of the hiring practices of some of the best-run companies were obtained from the materials they shared with me. An article by entitled "What's New in Employment Testing" that appeared on p. 17 of *The New York Times Magazine* on Sunday, February 24, 1985 was also extremely beneficial.

Lesson 7: Establish a Holistic Relationship with the Community

Robert Levering, Milton Moskowitz, and Michael Katz's *The 100 Best Companies to Work for in America* (Reading, Mass: Addison-Wesley, 1984) was an invaluable guide in preparing this chapter. The materials submitted to me by the companies mentioned in this lesson also proved extremely helpful, as did the Hallmark magazine, *Crown*, December 1984, Vol. 8, No. 5, p. 21. William Ouchi's book, *Theory Z* (Reading; Mass: Addison-Wesley, 1981) helped me to understand "holism" better.

Lesson 8: Disseminate an Informative Annual Report

All of the information about the annual reports of the companies cited was obtained from materials these companies shared with me. I also found an article by Todd S.

Purdum entitled "What's New in Annual Reports" which appeared on p. 17 *The New York Times* on Sunday, April 21, 1985 interesting and informative.

Lesson 9: Establish Circles of Excellence

Most of the substance for this chapter came from one of my books, *Improving Productivity in Schools by Using Quality Circles* (New York: The Institute for Advancing Educational Management, 1983).

Lesson 10: Create an Atmosphere of Caring, Intimacy, and Trust

Much of the substance for this lesson came from my book *Excellent Organizations* (Westbury, N.Y.: J. L. Wilkerson, 1985), pp. 9-55. I am very grateful to the numerous people of the best-run companies who shared their materials and stories with me. I made use of information from Thomas Peters and Nancy Austin's *A Passion for Excellence* (New York: Random House, 1985), pp. 265-293. The idea for the pledge statement came from Joe Batten's book *Expectations and Possibilities* (Reading, Mass: Addison-Wesley, 1981), pp. 79-81.

Lesson 11: Manage by Wandering Around

The substance of this lesson was taken from Thomas J. Peters and Nancy Austin's book, *A Passion for Excellence* (New York: Random House, 1985), p. 323. I also made use of the materials sent to me by many of the best-run companies and of my book *Excellent Organizations* (Westbury, N.Y.: J. L. Wilkerson, 1985).

Lesson 12: Establish a Succession Program

My ideas for this lesson came from Harry Levinson and Stuart Rosenthal's *CEO* (New York: Basic Books, 1984) and from reading several Management Reviews published monthly by the American Management Association.

Lesson 13: Address the Whole Person

The substance of this lesson was obtained from Robert Levering, Milton Moskowitz, and Michael Katz's *The 100 Best Companies to Work for in America* (Reading, Mass: Addison-Wesley, 1984). I also made good use of some of the materials some of the best-run companies sent to me about their respective wellness programs. I am also indebted to Dean Grant for sharing information about his school district's life-assessment program.

Glossary

Autonomy. The power to decide for oneself how one is going to manage an entire process.

Career-Path Program. A long-range plan for providing successive on-the-job learning experiences involving a variety of functions, geared to improving an employee's skills and value to the organization.

Certified Quality Circle Facilitator. A person who has completed a minimum of five days or forty hours of comprehensive training under a certified facilitator in the various phases of the quality circle concept and has passed an extensive examination.

Circle Leader. An employee, usually a unit supervisor, who has been trained in the quality circle concept and provides leadership to circle members as they work to solve problems.

Circle Members. Employees trained in the quality circle concept who work together to solve job-related problems. Consensus. A decision-making process whereby members of a team or group arrive at a mutually acceptable decision which all participants agree to support.

Culture. An integrated pattern of human behavior that is exhibited by an identifiable group of people and includes thought, speech, action, and artifacts. Entrepreneurship. The process of developing innovative principles, practices, and products outside the confines of any established organization.

213

General School Administrator. A school administrator, usually on the central administration level, who has had at least one year of actual experience in the areas of personnel, business administration, curriculum, and instructional administration.

Inculcating the philosophy. The process of impressing upon people certain macroprinciples governing behavior and attitudes.

Intrapreneurship. The process of developing innovative principles, practices, programs, and products *within* an established organization.

Job Rotation. A formal plan for assigning employees to different jobs so they can get training in a variety of functions.

Mission. The general purpose of an organization.

Nominal Group Process. A method of organizing a group's interactions that allows group members maximum involvement in the making of decisions.

Performance Evaluation. A critical assessment of work performed, conducted formally or informally by an individual or group.

Quality Circle. A group of three to eleven persons who meet voluntarily, usually for one hour a week, to identify, analyze, and devise solutions to job-related problems in the group's area of responsibility; verify the solutions; recommend them to superiors; and implement them when possible.

Shared Values Statement. A statement identifying the values that are or should be held by all members of an organization.

Statement of Philosophy. A document that spells out the socio- economic purposes, mission, beliefs, and goals of an organization.

Training. An organized activity designed to improve an employee's job performance and therefore his or her value to the organization.

Training Strand. A continuum of training activities designed to prepare an employee to perform one or more specific functions.

Bibliography

Ash, Mary Kay. *Mary Kay on People Management.* New York: Warner Books, 1984.

Auvine, Brian, Betsy Densmore, Mary Extron, Scott Paole, and Michael Shanklin. *A Manual for Group Facilitators.* Madison, Wis.: The Center for Conflict Resolution, 1978.

Avery, Michael, Brian Auvine, Barbara Streibel, and Lennie Weiss. *Building United Judgment: A Handbook for Consensus Decision Making.* Madison, Wis.: The Center for Conflict Resolution, 1981.

Bartov, Glenn. *Decisions by Consensus.* Chicago: Progressive Publisher, 1978.

Bennett, Dudley. *TA and the Manager.* New York: AMACOM, 1976.

Blakeslee, Thomas R. *The Right Brain: A New Understanding of the Unconscious Mind and Its Creative Power.* Garden City, N.Y.: Anchor Press/Doubleday, 1980.

Blanchard, Kenneth and Spencer Johnson. *The One-Minute Manager.* New York: William Morrow, 1982.

Blanchard, Kenneth, Patricia Zigarmi, and Drea Zigarmi. *Leadership and the One-Minute Manager.* New York: William Morrow, 1985.

Christopher, William F. *Management for the 1980's.* New York: AMACOM, 1980.

Cribbin, James J. *Leadership —Strategies for Organizational Effectiveness*. New York: AMACOM, 1981.

Cribbin, James J. *Leadership—Your Competitive Edge*. New York: AMACOM, 1981.

Cummings, Paul W. *Open Management: Guides to Successful Practice*. New York: AMACOM, 1980.

Deal, Terrence E., and Allan A. Kennedy. *Corporate Cultures: The Rites and Rituals of Corporate Life*. Reading, Mass.: Addison-Wesley, 1982.

Delbecq, Andre L., Andrew Van de Ven, and David H. Gustafson. *Group Techniques for Program Planning: A Guide to Nominal Group and Delphi Processes*. Glenview, Ill.: Scott Foresman, 1975.

Dreyfack, Raymond. *Making It in Management: The Japanese Way*. Rockville Centre, N. Y.: Farnsworth, 1982.

Drucker, Peter F. *Innovation and Entrepreneurship—Practice and Principles*. New York: Harper & Row, 1985.

Feinberg, Mortimer, Robert Tanofsky, and John J. Tarrant. *The New Psychology for Managing People*. Englewood Cliffs, N.J., Prentice-Hall, 1978.

Gardner, James E. *Training the New Supervisor*. New York: AMACOM, 1980.

Geneen, Harold D. *Managing*. New York: Doubleday, 1984.

Gilder, George. *The Spirit of Enterprise*. New York: Simon & Schuster, 1984.

Goldberg, Philip. *The Intuitive Edge: Understanding and Developing Intuition.* Los Angeles: J. P. Tarcher, 1983.

Hickman, Craig R., and Michael A. Silva. *Creating Excellence—Managing Corporate Culture, Strategy, and Change in the New Age.* New York: New American Library, 1984.

Hughes, Charles L. *Goal Setting: Key to Individual and Organizational Effectiveness.* New York: American Management Association, 1965.

Iacocca, Lee. *Iacocca—An Autobiography.* New York: Bantam Books, 1984.

Ingle, Sud. *Quality Circles Master Guide.* Englewood Cliffs, N.J.: Prentice-Hall, 1982.

Iwata, Ryushi. *Japanese Style Management: Its Foundation and Prospects.* Tokyo: Asian Productivity Organization, 1982.

Kanter, Rosabeth Moss. *The Change Masters— Innovation and Entrepreneurship in the American Corporation.* New York: Simon & Schuster, 1983.

Kelsey, Morton T. *Caring—How Can We Love One Another?* New York: Paulist Press, 1981.

Keyes, Ken, Jr. *Handbook to Higher Consciousness.* Marina del Rey, Calif.: De Vorss, 1975.

Knowles, Malcolm, and Knowles, Hulda. *Introduction to Group Dynamics.* Chicago: Association Press, 1972.

Kotter, John P. *The General Managers.* New York: The Free Press, 1982.

Krathwohl, David R., Benjamin S. Bloom, and Bertram

B. Masia. *Taxonomy of Educational Objectives. The Classification of Educational Goals. Handbook II: Affective Domain.* New York: David McKay, 1956.

Leavitt, Harold J. *Managerial Psychology.* Chicago: The University of Chicago Press, 1964.

LeBoeuf, Michael. *The Greatest Management Principle in the World.* New York: G. P. Putnam's Sons, 1985.

Lee, Sang M. *Management by Multiple Objectives: A Modern Management Approach.* New York: Petrocelli Books, 1981.

Levering, Robert, Milton Moskowitz, and Michael Katz. *The 100 Best Companies to Work for in America.* Reading, Mass.: Addison-Wesley, 1984.

Levinson, Harry, and Stuart Rosenthal. *CEO: Corporate Leadership in Action.* New York: Basic Books, 1984.

McCormack, Mark H. *What They Don't Teach You at Harvard Business School.* New York: Bantam Books, 1984.

Miller, Lawrence M. *American Spirit—Visions of a New Corporate Culture.* New York: William Morrow, 1984.

Mink, Oscar, James M. Schultz, and Barbara P. Mink. *Developing and Managing Open Organizations.* Austin, Tex.: Learning Concepts, 1979.

Myers, M. Scott. *Every Employee a Manager.* New York: McGraw- Hill, 1981.

Nadler, Leonard. *Developing Human Resources.* Austin, Tex.: Learning Concepts, 1970.

Ohmae, Kenichi. *The Mind of the Strategist.* New York: McGraw-Hill, 1982.

Ouchi, William. *Theory Z: How American Business Can Meet the Japanese Challenge.* Reading, Mass.: Addison-Wesley, 1981.

Pascale, Richard T., and Anthony G. Athos. *The Art of Japanese Management: Applications for American Executives.* New York: Simon & Schuster, 1981.

Peters, Thomas J., and Nancy Austin. *A Passion for Excellence—The Leadership Difference.* New York: Random House, 1985.

Peters, Thomas J., and Robert H. Waterman. *In Search of Excellence: Lessons from America's Best-Run Companies.* New York: Harper & Row, 1982.

Pinchot, Gifford, III. *Intrapreneuring. Why You Don't Have to Leave the Corporation to Become an Entrepreneur.* New York: Harper & Row, 1985.

QC Circle Headquarters. *QC Circle Koryo—General Principles of the QC Circle.* San Jose, Calif.: QC Circle Headquarters, 1980.

Quick, Thomas L. *Person to Person Management.* New York: St. Martin's Press, 1977.

Randolph, Robert M. *Planagement—Moving Concept into Reality.* New York: AMACOM, 1974.

Schonberger, Richard J. *Japanese Manufacturers' Techniques: Nine Hidden Lessons in Simplicity.* New York: The Free Press, 1982.

Short, James H. *Working in Teams: Practical Manual for Improving Work Groups.* New York: AMACOM, 1981.

Steiner, George A. *Strategies Planning: What Every*

Manager Must Know. New York: The Free Press, 1979.

Toffler, Alvin, *The Adaptive Corporation.* New York: McGraw- Hill, 1985.

Toole, James, *Vanguard Management —Redesigning the Corporate Future.* Garden City, N.Y.: Doubleday, 1985.

Tregoe, Benjamin B., and John B. Zimmerman. *Top Management Strategy.* New York: Simon & Schuster, 1980.

AMAX, 175
Absenteeism; in business, 8; in schools, 15, 24, 26–27, 68, 70, 123, 200
Academic achievement, 24, 27, 186
Achieving Excellence in Our Schools, xiii-xiv, xxi, 74, 125
Administration circles, 134. *See also* Circles of excellence; teams
Administrators, school, passim; certification of, 185
Advanced Micro Devices, 20–21, 75–76
Alcoholism, 18, 150, 194, 196
Aldikacti, Hulki, xiii
Allen, Robert, 64
American Association of School Administrators, 190
American Management Association, 124, 178, 190
American Society for Training and Development, 190
Apple Computer, 20, 32, 55, 95, 97, 116–117, 155
Armstrong World Industries, 38, 53
Association for Fitness in Business, 204–205
Association for Supervision and Curriculum Development, 144
Atari, 9–10
Atlantic City (NJ), 110
Atlantic Richfield, 105
Audiovisual aids, xix 145. *See also* Displays, graphs, videotape
Austin, Nancy, xxi, 1, 7, 149, 155, 163
Autonomy; in business organizations, 18; in schools, 22, 26, 59, 74, 125
Awards, 35, 46, 54, 105, 110–111, 120, 123–124, 145, 174, 201
Awareness training, 136, 143. *See also* Training

Baseline data, 193, 200

Caspersen, Finn, 63
Cause-and-effect diagrams, 139
Celestial Seasonings, 39–40, 54, 91, 155
Certification. *See* Administrators; teachers
Champions; in business, 17; in communities, 109; in schools (teaching), 13, 82, 124
Change, 2–4, 6, 82–83, 85
Chief executive officer, 18–19, 38, 52–53, 61–62, 64–65, 97, 99, 148, 154, 175, 198
Child; abuse, 105, 107; care, 52–53
Cincinnati Business Committee, 108
Circles of excellence, 72, 76, 82, 85, 125–145, 180; definition, 126. *See also* Administration circles; joint circles
Citicorp, 54, 175
Collective bargaining, 133
College entrance, 119
Colleges and universities, xxii–xxiii, 74
Color printing for reports, 114–115
Commercial Credit, 204
Committees, 15, 33, 86–87, 103, 105, 107–108, 130, 152, 185–187, 191; steering, 135–136, 144
Communication, xx, 1, 5, 15, 22, 53, 59, 62, 69, 113–124, 128, 130, 134, 143, 153–154, 167–171, 179–180, 199. *See also* Newsletters
Community relations; of businesses, 50; of schools, xxviii, 85, 101–112, 118, 121
Competition in business, 29, 46
Computers, xxvii, 20, 26, 53, 61–72, 74, 79, 116, 120–121, 197; as calendars, 63, 66, 68; as communicators, 64, 66; as data files, 65, 138, 196; as writers, 63; Macintosh, 116–117
Consensus; in business, 35, 45, 155–156; in schools, xxvii, 13, 16, 22, 65, 68, 96–97, 161, 179, 184

Incentives, 8, 35, 54. *See also* Awards
Inequalities, 34–35
Information, 5, 12. *See also* Communication
Innovation, xvi, 22, 32, 73–87
Interest test, 94, 186
International; Association of Quality Circles, 134; Institute of Intrapreneurs, 181
Internship, 90
Interviewing, 85–86, 92, 94–96, 99, 186
Intimacy in organization management, 151–154
Intrapreneurship, 5, 125
Japanese, 33
Jenkins, George, 36–37, 55–56
Job; descriptions, 23, 51, 161; rotation, 180; satisfaction, 35, 135, 142
John F. Kennedy High School (N.Y.C.), 105
Johnson & Johnson, 55, 196
Joint circles of excellence, 133–134

Kansas City, 107
Kanter, Rosabeth Moss, 73
Keeblor, Richard O., 204
Ketelson, James L., 105–106
Kollmorgen Corporation, 16, 97, 152–153, 155
Kotter, John, xviii

Lapur, Mitchell, xvii
Lateness; in business, 8; in schools, 15
Lay-offs in business, 18, 39
Leadership, 85, 136–137, 199–200
Learning; administrator's, 180; individualized, 68; student, 81, 120–122
Lehr, Lewis W., 43
Leo Burnett Company, 52, 54

Orientation programs, 97, 161
Ouchi, William, 103
Overtime, 49
Ownership (responsibility) in schools, xxviii, 1–16, 199
Oxford English Dictionary, 30

PSAT, 120
Packard, David, 163
Parents, 86, 102, 109, 154, 173–174
Pareto charts, 139
Parker-Sharpe (H.), Inc., 93
Parking spaces, 38, 59
Pascarella, Perry, 29
Passion for Excellence, A, xiv, 155, 163–164
Peer reviews, 184
Pensions, 49, 122
People Express, 7–8, 16, 32, 156
Perdue, Frank, 172
Performance review. *See* Review of performance
Perks (privileges); of employees, 35; of management, 32
Personality; conflicts, 133; test, 93, 99, 186
Personnel department (human resources department), 177, 180, 182, 185
Peters, Tom, xiv, xvi, xxi, 1, 7, 17, 23, 149, 155, 163
Philosophy, statement of; in business, 95, 97, 117, 172; in schools, xviii–xix, 24–25, 90–91, 110
Physical fitness, 55, 150, 194–198
Pickens, T. Boone, 198
Planning, 12–13, 25, 58, 69–71, 111, 164, 187–189, 200
Planning Executives Institute, 181
Pledge of excellence, 158–160
Political equality, 30, 45
Politics, 177
Population shifts, 83

circles of excellence, 140, 145. *See also* Dissemination of reports

Research and development, xv, vii, 73–87, 121, 123, 156, 180; definition, 80–81

Respect among employees and managers; in business, 36, 38–39, 51–53, 157; in schools, 57

Retirement; awards, 35; compensation plan, 62

Review of performance; in business, 18; in schools, 183–184, 189–190

Robertson, H. H., 9

Rogers, Carl, 169

Role; model, xix, 94; playing, 14, 172

Rolm Corporation, 49

Rosenthal, Stuart, 175

SAT scores, xv, 69, 119–120, 123

Safety, 10, 39, 55, 57, 150

Sales; and marketing, 133; persons, 7; quotas, 18, 21; research, 77

Scholarships, xxiii, 42

School; districts, passim; management, xv, passim

Schools; elementary, 11, 26; high, 22, 26, 105, 164; intermediate, 134; junior high, 134; public and private, 21, 73, 174; small-scale, 22

Secretary, 66–68

Security addiction, 3–4

Security Pacific Corporation, 130–131

Selection of personnel, 25. *See also* Teachers

Self-; actualization, 39–40, 57–58, 127; confidence, 47, 130; esteem, 57, 125, 127; management, 13, 52

Seminars, 2, 14, 79

Shanker, Albert, 89–90, 98

Sick-leave, 52. *See also* Medical care

Silva, Michael A., xix

Smale, John G., 41–42
Smart-dumb rule, 23
Smoking, 194, 196
Social Benefits Program, 112
Social worker, 101–103
Software, xvii, 65, 68–71, 78
Sony Corporation, xvii
Speaking, xix, 92, 95, 179–180, 182
Spread sheets, 69–70, 72
Stakeholders' analysis, 111, 113, 119, 122, 172–174
Staley, Phil, 166
Stamper, Malcolm, 62–64
State departments of education, 25, 74, 190. *See also* New Jersey State Department of Education
Status, disparities in, 34, 60
Stay-Well Program, 196–198
Stock ownership by employees, 9, 49, 54, 150
Students, xv–xvi, xxii–xxiv, xxvi, 1, 23–24, 26, 28, 61, 74, 81, 84–85, 89, 101–103, 116, 119–120, 154, 173–174, 200–201
Sublimity statement; in business, 50–51; in schools, 60
Substitute teachers, 12
Succession, 37–38, 98, 175–191. *See also* Four-Tier Comprehensive Succession Program
Superintendents, school, xiv–xv, xxi, 3, 11, 13, 25, 59, 61, 65–71, 75, 113, 118–119, 122, 123–124, 144, 147–149, 154, 158, 163, 177, 179, 181, 188, 198
Surveys, 56–58, 82
Syntex Corporation, 167
Tandem Computer, 166
Teachers, xiii, xxiv–xxv, 1, 3, 10–13, 16, 23–24, 26–28, 60, 74, 81, 84–87, 144, 153–155, 161, 165, 174, 183–184, 194, 199; certification of, 90–91; selection of, 89–99. *See also* Substitute teachers

Teaching, 21, 74, 121

Teagle, Walter, 175

Teams; in business, 8–9, 20, 29, 39, 50, 53, 77, 125–145, 157; in schools, xxii, xxvii, 6, 13–16, 21–22, 74, 86, 94–96, 98, 124, 125–145, 162, 164, 177, 181, 183, 191, 197, 203; option, 129–130; participative, 129–130; react, 129–130

Tenneco, Inc., 105–106, 196, 205

Termination, 133

Tesla, Nikola, xvi–xvii

Testing; in business, 76–77; in schools, 81, 120; of teachers, 89–90, 92–95, 97–98. *See also* Interest test; personality test

Thanks, xxvii, 11, 171

Thanksgiving, 102–103

Thorston Temparament Schedule, 99

3M, 19, 40, 43, 79–80, 85, 148, 156, 175

Time, Inc., 49

Time clocks, 49, 51, 155, 161

Titles; in business, 32, 34, 44; in schools, 59, 162

Tolerance of mistakes; in business, 17; in schools, 59

Tore, Reginald H., 175

Training; in business, 39–41, 46, 53, 77, 91, 129, 151, 163; in computer use, 66; in schools, xxv, 26, 28, 59, 68, 71, 92–93, 97–98, 120, 123, 127, 130, 144, 159, 176, 178, 181, 184, 186–190. *See also* Awareness training

Training and Development Journal, 190

Trammell Crow Company, 34, 152, 155

Treybig, Jimmy, 166

Trust, 11–12, 51, 134, 147–162, 165

Trust House Forte, 8

Tuechtner, W. Matthew, 193

Tupperware, 7

Turner, Ted, 116